BOOK 4

KEY STAGE 3
Mathematics
FOR NORTHERN IRELAND

James Boston

Kate Johnston

Audrey Moody

Series Editor Miriam McMullan
Series Consultant Lowry Johnston

HODDER
EDUCATION
AN HACHETTE UK COMPANY

Acknowledgements

The Publishers would like to thank the following for permission to reproduce copyright material:
p46 Istock (robin); p81 shutterstock (triskelion); p81 Istock (recycling symbol); p81 Istock (snowflake); p81 Istock (wheel); p81 Istock (playing card); p82 Sun Microsystems logo: Sun, Sun Microsystems, and the Sun Logo are trademarks or registered trademarks of Sun Microsystems, Inc. in the United States and other countries; p92 Istock (car); p92. Lipót Fejér's house: www.pecsiapartman.hu
Photography © Zsuzsa Nun; p96 Istock (cloud); p100 Istock (Antrim tower); p106 Istock (Penny Farthing); p153 Photolibrary (Giant's Causeway); p157 Istock (feathers); p157 Istock (lead); p157 Shutterstock (Dead Sea); p174 Istock (computer).

Every effort has been made to trace all copyright holders, but if any have been inadvertently overlooked the Publishers will be pleased to make the necessary arrangements at the first opportunity.

Although every effort has been made to ensure that website addresses are correct at time of going to press, Hodder Education cannot be held responsible for the content of any website mentioned in this book. It is sometimes possible to find a relocated web page by typing in the address of the home page for a website in the URL window of your browser.

Hachette UK's policy is to use papers that are natural, renewable and recyclable products and made from wood grown in sustainable forests. The logging and manufacturing processes are expected to conform to the environmental regulations of the country of origin.

Orders: please contact Bookpoint Ltd, 130 Milton Park, Abingdon, Oxon OX14 4SB. Telephone: (44) 01235 827720. Fax: (44) 01235 400454. Lines are open 9.00 – 5.00, Monday to Saturday, with a 24-hour message answering service. Visit our website at www.hoddereducation.co.uk

© James Boston, Kate Johnston, Audrey Moody, Miriam McMullan 2009
First published in 2009 by
Hodder Education,
An Hachette UK Company
338 Euston Road
London NW1 3BH

Impression number   5 4 3 2 1
Year   2012 2011 2010 2009

Cover photo © Cocoon/Getty
Illustrations by Peters and Zabransky Ltd and Stephen May.
Typeset in Futura Book 11/14pt by Starfish Design Editorial and Project Management Ltd.
Printed and bound in Italy

A catalogue record for this title is available from the British Library

ISBN: 978 0340 92715 1

Contents

Introduction

This series has been written specifically for the Key Stage 3 Curriculum for Northern Ireland.

Book 4 provides opportunities to develop the mathematical skills and understanding you will need if you are working at Level 6 of the Progression in Using Mathematics across the Curriculum levels (with the introduction of a number of Level 7 topics). This is achieved through a wide variety of learning approaches, including discussions, examples, exercises, consolidation practice, practical activities and Tasks.

This Pupil's Book provides opportunities to:

- Cover the Key Elements for Mathematics with Financial Capability.

- Develop Thinking Skills and Personal Capabilities.

- Develop the skill of Using ICT.

- Develop Mental Mathematics skills.

- Complete exercises with and without using a calculator.

Key Elements

The Key Elements for Mathematics with Financial Capability in Book 4 are met in the following ways.

1	Personal understanding	• Investigate ways in which we spend our time.
2	Mutual understanding	• Show respect for others' views when working in a group or in class discussions.
3	Personal health	• Investigate how choices about food and exercise affect our health. • Carry out experiments and analyse data relating to health issues.
4	Moral character	• Provide a reasoned solution to questions.
5	Spiritual awareness	• Investigate patterns in nature.
6	Citizenship	• Find out how you can get involved in issues that affect your school, your local area and the wider world through mathematical data.
7	Cultural understanding	• Explore the contributions of different cultures to mathematics.
8	Media awareness	• Examine the use and misuse of mathematics in the media. • Interpret data used by the media.

9 Ethical awareness	•	Look at statistics in relation to social issues.
10 Employability	•	Examine the role of mathematics as a 'key' to your future education, training and employment.
	•	Explore how the skills developed through mathematics will be useful in a range of careers.
11 Economic awareness	•	Apply mathematical skills in real-life situations linking with financial capability.
12 Education for sustainable development	•	Understand the need to manage renewable and non-renewable resources.
	•	Investigate the various costs and benefits of waste management.

The opportunities for the key elements of Thinking Skills and Personal Capabilities are indicated by the following icons.

Skill	Icon	Description
Managing information		• Research and manage information relating to mathematical situations, including collecting and recording primary data, interpreting a range of secondary sources such as tables, charts, diagrams and graphs.
		• Analyse and carry out calculations for sets of data and present findings using paper methods or with ICT packages.
Thinking, problem solving, decision making		• Show deeper mathematical understanding by generating possible outcomes, suggesting alternative approaches and evaluating methods chosen.
		• Make links with mathematical knowledge and other situations.
Being creative		• Develop the ability to generate appropriate questions to define problems and be able to suggest a variety of strategies for their solution.
		• Develop the individual's confidence in his or her approach.
Working with others		• Work effectively in pairs or in a group, valuing the contribution of others.
Self-management		• Work independently to manage, evaluate and improve own learning.

Negative numbers

In this chapter, I am learning to:

- use negative numbers in context
- add, subtract, multiply and divide negative numbers
- use BODMAS to calculate with negative numbers
- understand squares and cubes of negative numbers.

Discussion 1.1

Julie has £300 in the bank at the start of July. During the month she spends £550. What is the balance of her account at the end of July?

At the start of September she has a balance of –£35. She puts £80 into her account but spends £60. What is the balance of her account now?

Connor wants to start budgeting and decides to keep a spreadsheet showing his expenditure and balance every week. Work with a partner to copy and complete the table to show the balance of his account each week.

Week number	Balance	Money in	Money out
1	– £140	£85	£55
2	– £110	£80	£40
3		£90	£110
4		£75	£45
5		–	–

Exercise 1a

1   James has £120 in the bank. He spends £53 on a duvet cover and £97 on a pair of curtains. What is his bank balance now?

2 Kathryn keeps a record of her bank balance each week.
Copy the table and complete the missing balances.

Money in	Money out	Balance
£72	£0	£72
£30	£110	
£0	£55	

3 Part of Mrs Armstrong's bank balance sheet is shown.

Deposit/Withdrawal	Balance
£0	–£325
–£45	
	£500

Copy the table and complete the two missing entries.

Discussion 1.2

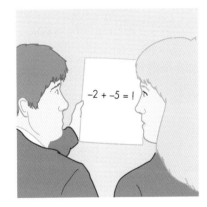

Kathryn and Niall are working out the answer to some questions involving negative numbers. The first question is:

–2 + –5

Kathryn says, 'This question is the same as –2 – 5 which gives –7'.

Niall says 'Start at –2 on the number line and move 5 places to the left on the number line'. He also calculates that the answer is –7.

The next question is

+ 3 – + 7

What calculation would you do using Kathryn's method? What is the answer?

Using Niall's method, describe how you could use a number line to find the answer.

The next question is: –2 – – 5

Kathryn says, 'This question is the same as –2 + 5 which gives + 3'.
Using Niall's method, describe how you might use a number line to find the answer.

Use a calculator to check the answers to each question.

Exercise 1b

1 Find the answers to these without using a calculator.

   a 3 + –4   **b** –2 – +3   **c** –5 + –10

   d 8 – –2   **e** –5 – –4   **f** –6 – +7

   g +4 – +4   **h** 11 – –11   **i** 7 + –8

   j –7 – +8

2 At the end of one month Kerry works out how much money she has in the bank. She writes down the calculation she needs to do using '–' for amounts that she has spent that month and '+' for amounts that she deposited in the bank.

   348 + (–87) + (+76) + (–103) + (–56) + (–21) + (–17) + (–121)

   The first value of £348 is the amount she had in the bank at the start of the month.

   How much money does Kerry have at the end of the month?

Discussion 1.3

One way of working out 3 × –2 is shown.

3 × –2 = (–2) + (–2) + (–2) = –6

Using the same method, what are the answers to 4 × –3? 3 × –5   –7 × +2?   –4 × +4?

Discuss with a partner how you could finish this sentence:

When a positive number is multiplied by a negative number, the answer will be a _____ number.

We know that 3 × –2 = –6.

What do you think the answer to –3 × –2 will be?

What are the answers to: –3 × –5? –7 × –2?   –4 × –4?

Discuss with a partner how you could finish this sentence:

When a negative number is multiplied by a negative number, the answer will be a _____ number.

Exercise 1c

1 Copy and complete the calculations.

a $4 \times -8 =$ b $-6 \times -3 =$ c $-5 \times 3 =$

d $4 \times -6 =$ e $-2 \times -7 =$ f $-8 \times +3 =$

g $+7 \times -5 =$ h $-5 \times -5 =$ i $-7 \times +3 =$

j $-4 \times -3 =$ k $+6 \times -7 =$

2 Copy and complete this multiplication square.

×	−2	+5	−10	+12
+3				
−4				
−6				
+10				

3 In a quiz, questions are worth 2, 3 or 5 points depending on difficulty. If a team gets the question wrong, they score −2, −3 or −5 points.

The table shows the number of each type of question that Team A got right or wrong during the quiz.

Team A	2-point questions	3-point questions	5-point questions
Number right	6	3	0
Number wrong	3	5	3

a How many points did Team A score altogether?

The table for Team B is shown.

Team B	2-point questions	3-point questions	5-point questions
Number right	5	7	2
Number wrong	1	3	2

b How many points did Team B score altogether?

c Team C scored −4 points altogether. There were only three teams in the quiz. Which team came last?

Discussion 1.4

We have seen that $3 \times -2 = -6$ so, using inverse operations, $-6 \div 3 = -2$.

What are the answers to $-6 \div -2$ $-10 \div 5$ $-8 \div -4$?

What can you say about the rules for multiplying positive and negative numbers and the rules for dividing positive and negative numbers?

**Activity
Sheet 1.1**

Activity 1.1

Exercise 1d

1 Find the value of:

   a $12 \div -6$ b $-8 \div -8$ c $-9 \div 3$ d $15 \div -5$

   e $-15 \div -5$ f $-15 \div 5$ g $-18 \div -6$ h $24 \div -8$

   i $-15 \div 2$ j $2 \div -4$

2 Complete the division square by dividing the numbers in the first row by the numbers in the first column.

÷	−10	+15	−12	−20
−5				
+2				
+5				
+10				

**Activity
Sheet 1.2**

Activity 1.2

Discussion 1.5

What does $(-3)^2$ mean? Use your calculator to find the value of $(-3)^2$. Remember to include the brackets.

Without using a calculator, calculate the answer to $(-5)^2$.

Eva and Niamh are working out the answer to -2^2.

Eva says that it means that you square -2.

$-2^2 = -2 \times -2 = +4$

Niamh says that it means that you square 2 and then put a $-$ sign in front of it.

$-2^2 = -(2 \times 2) = -4$

Who do you think is right? Use a calculator to help you decide.

Which of these gives a different answer from the other two?

-4^2 $(-4)^2$ $-(4)^2$

Exercise 1e

1 Find the value of:

   a 6^2 **b** $(+6)^2$

   c $+6^2$ **d** -6 squared

   e $(-6)^2$ **f** -7^2

   g -5^2 **h** $(-4)^2$

   i $(-10)^2$ **j** $-(5$ squared$)$

2 Which of these statements are true?

   a $-9^2 = -81$ **b** $9 \times 9 = (-9)^2$

   c $5^2 = (-5)^2$ **d** $-7 \times 7 = 7^2$

   e $-(10)^2 = 10 \times -10$ **f** $(-a)^2 = -a^2$

3 Find the value of:

   a $(-3)^2 - 5^2$ **b** 2 squared $-$ 4 squared

   c $4^2 - 6^2$ **d** $-3^2 - (-3)^2$

   e $-3^2 - (-3^2)$ **f** $3^2 + -3^2$

   g $(-4)^2 - (-5)^2$ **h** $(-4)^2 + (-5)^2$

Example 1.1

What is the value of 2^3?

$2^3 = 2 \times 2 \times 2 = 8$

What about $(-2)^3$? Is this the same as -2^3?

$(-2^3) = -2 \times -2 \times -2 = +4 \times -2 = -8$

$\quad -2^3 = -(2 \times 2 \times 2) = -8$

The answers are the same.

Exercise 1f

1 Find the value of:

    a -3^3 **b** $(-3)^3$ **c** -4^3

    d $(-5)^3$ **e** -10 cubed   **f** $(-4)^3$

2 Which of these statements are true?

    a $-10^3 = (-10)^3$ **b** $-2^3 + 2^3 = 0$

    c $3 \times (-3)^2 = (-3)^3$ **d** $-3 \times (-3)^2 = (-3)^3$

    e $-(-4)$ cubed $= -64$

3 Find the value of:

    a -3 cubed $+ -2$ cubed   **b** $-3^3 - -2^3$

    c $(-10)^3 - -10^3$ **d** $4^3 - (-4)^3$

Discussion 1.6

Ryan wants to find the answer to $-6 + 4 \times -2$ without using a calculator.

He thinks the answer is either $+4$ or -14 but he doesn't know which is correct.

How do you think Ryan got these two answers? Which answer is correct?

The word 'BODMAS' reminds us to do calculations in the correct order.

B – brackets
O – order (or index)
D – division
M – multiplication
A – addition
S – subtraction

Example 1.2

What is the value of $(-2)^3 + 3(-12 \div -6) - 14$?

Do the calculation in **brackets** first

$(-2)^3 + 3(-12 \div -6) - 14 = (-2)^3 + 3 \times 2 - 14$

Then **order** (or index)

$(-2)^3 + 3 \times 2 - 14 = -8 + 3 \times 2 - 14$

Then **multiplication**

$-8 + 3 \times 2 - 14 = -8 + 6 - 14$

Then **addition** as it comes before subtraction when working from left to right in this calculation

$-8 + 6 - 14 = -2 - 14$

Finally **subtraction** $-2 - 14 = -16$

Exercise 1g

1 Find the value of:

a $-2 + 3 \times -4$ b $4 \times -3 + 2 \times -5$

c $12 - 15 \div -5 + 3$ d $-4 + (-3)^2 \times 2$

e $5 - 2^3 + 4(6 - 2^3)$ f $20 - (3^3 - 5^2) + 2 \times (-2)^2$

g $6 \times -3 + 4^2 \div -2 - 8$ h $18 + 20 \div 4 + (5 - 3)^3$

i $(-6)^2 \div (-3)^2 \times -5$ j $100 - 72 - 3(4^2 - 2^3)^2 + 4 \times -5$

2 Copy and complete these calculations.

a $\underline{} \times -3 = -27$ b $-42 \div \underline{} = 7$

c $-6 - \underline{} = 2$ d $3 \times \underline{} \times -2 = -18$

e $-8 - \underline{} = 0$ f $-8 - \underline{} = -16$

g $-2 + 3 \times \underline{} = -14$ h $10 - (5 - \underline{}) = -1$

i $-21 \div (7 \times \underline{}) = 3$ j $10 \times -3 + \underline{} \times -2 = -12$

Exercise 1h

Find the value of:

1 3.7×-0.01

2 $-2.6 + 16.32 \times -3.5$

3 $1.2 - 8.5 \div -5 + 2.8$

4 $(-0.7)^2 \times 1.2^3$

5 $2.7^3 + 0.8(1.1 - 3.2^3)$

6 $-(0.32^3 - 0.14^2) + (-0.4)^2$

7 $16.8 \times -1.4 \div -2 - 31.9$

8 $7.82 \div 1.7 + (21.7 - 23.4)^3$

9 $(-6.4)^2 \div (-4)^3 - (-3.7 + 4.3)$

10 $100.4 - 3.1(0.8^2 - 2.3^3)^2 + 11.42 \times -5.1$

Consolidation Exercise

1 Copy and complete these calculations.

a $-4 \times -3 =$ **b** $-7 + -6 =$ **c** $-12 \div 6 =$

d $-7 + 3 - 10 =$ **e** $+ 8 \times -3 =$ **f** $-2^3 =$

g $4 \times -2 \times -3 =$ **h** $(-4)^2 =$ **i** $5 - 7 - 9 =$

j $(-5)^3 =$ **k** $-7^2 - 5^2 =$ **l** $(-3) \times 2 - 33 =$

m $10^2 - (-10)^2 =$ **n** $-10^2 \div 10^2 =$

2 Copy and complete these calculations.

a $-6 \times \underline{\quad} = -12$ **b** $16 \div \underline{\quad} = -2$

c $-7 - \underline{\quad} = -3$ **d** $-7 \times \underline{\quad} = -35$

e $-8 + \underline{\quad} - 6 = + 14$ **f** $(\underline{\quad})^3 + 10 = -17$

g $19 - 14 - \underline{\quad} = 1$ **h** $4 \times 2 \times \underline{\quad} = -40$

3 Calculate

a $5 + 3 \times -4$ **b** $6 + -8 \div -2$

c $11 - (7 - 10) + (-3)^2$ **d** $40 \div 2 \times -4 - 1$

e $40 \div 2 \times (-4 - 1)$ **f** $40 \div (2 \times -4) - 1$

g $-6 + (-3)^2 - 2^3$ **h** $-4 - 3 \times -5 \times -2^2$

4 Kevin and Niall are playing a game to practise using negative numbers. They have a six-sided dice with the numbers 0, 1, –1, 2, –2 and –4 on the faces. They also have a four-sided spinner with +, –, ×, and ÷ on the edges.

To play the game, Kevin throws the dice and gets 1. He then spins the spinner and gets ×. He then throws the dice again and gets 2. He does the calculation 1 × 2, so his score is 2.

a What is the largest possible score?

b What is the smallest possible score?

c Write down all the possible ways to score –4.

d Write down all the possible ways to score zero.

2 Angles

In this chapter, I am learning to:

- use and understand the angle properties of polygons
- draw polygons using LOGO
- select appropriate equipment and construct triangles and simple scale drawings
- construct angle bisectors, 60° angles and perpendicular bisectors.

Discussion 2.1

What facts do you remember about parallel lines and angles?

Draw diagrams to help show each type of angle that you remember.

Activity Sheet 2.1

Activity 2.1

A **polygon** is a closed plane (two-dimensional) figure made up of three or more straight sides. Polygon A has four straight sides and four interior angles.

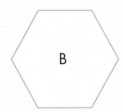

Regular polygons have sides of the same length, and all interior angles are equal. Polygons which are not regular are called **irregular** polygons. Polygon B is a regular hexagon. Polygon A is an irregular quadrilateral.

The **angle sum** of a polygon is the sum of its interior angles.

Discussion 2.2

What is the name of this polygon? Is it regular or irregular? Estimate the angle sum of this polygon.

Measure the interior angles with a protractor and find the angle sum. Check your answer with a friend. Why is it acceptable to have slightly different results?

Name other polygons. How many sides does each have?

Activity Sheet 2.2

Activity 2.2

Discussion 2.3

The angle sum of any triangle is 180°. What is the angle sum for any quadrilateral? How could you show that this result is true by using triangles? What is the least number of triangles a hexagon can be split into? (You may want to draw a diagram to help you.)

How does knowing the least number of triangles that the hexagon can be split into help you to find its angle sum?

Describe how to find the angle sum of a pentagon.

What is the relationship between the number of sides a polygon has and the least number of triangles it can be split into?

What is the angle sum of a 22-sided polygon?

The angle sum of a polygon is given as 2520°. How many sides does this polygon have? Explain your answer.

The **angle sum** of an *n*-sided polygon in degrees = $180 \times (n - 2)$.

Exercise 2a

Find the missing angles in the polygons. The diagrams are NOT drawn to scale.

a

80°

70°

a

b

45°

35°

b

40°

c

41°

133°

155°

78°

c

d

120°

270°

62°

d

100°

e

123°

94°

e

A polygon is shown with an interior and exterior angle labelled.

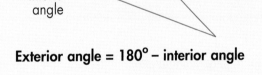

interior angle

exterior angle

Exterior angle = 180° − interior angle

Exercise 2b

1 Find the missing exterior angles.

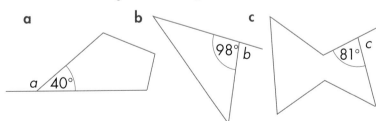

a

a 40°

b

98° b

c

81° c

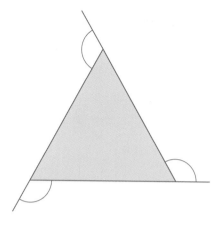

2 a An equilateral triangle is shown with its three exterior angles marked.

   i What size is each of the exterior angles?

   ii What is the sum of the exterior angles?

 b i Draw an irregular triangle and mark on the three exterior angles.

   ii Measure the exterior angles and find their sum.

 c i What size is each exterior angle of a square or rectangle?

   ii What is the sum of the exterior angles for squares and rectangles?

 d i Draw an irregular convex quadrilateral and mark on the exterior angles.

   ii What is the sum of the exterior angles for your quadrilateral?

3 a Draw an irregular convex pentagon and mark on its five exterior angles.

 b Measure each of the exterior angles and find their sum.

4 a Predict the sum of the exterior angles for a convex hexagon.

 b Draw a convex hexagon and measure the exterior angles to check your prediction.

 c Write a statement about exterior angles which is true for all convex polygons.

Activity Sheet 2.3

Activity 2.3

Discussion 2.4

Are all regular polygons convex? What is the exterior angle sum of any regular polygon? How could this information be used to *calculate* the size of an exterior angle of a regular decagon? What rule could you use to find the exterior angle of a regular n-sided polygon? When the exterior angle of a regular polygon is known, describe how the interior angle can be calculated.

Exercise 2c

1 a Copy and complete these statements.

   i Each exterior angle in a regular polygon = 360° ÷ _____

   ii interior angle = _____ – exterior angle

b Copy and complete the table for the sizes of interior and exterior angles in regular polygons.

Shape	Number of sides	Exterior angle	Interior angle
Equilateral triangle	3		
Square	4		
Pentagon	5		
Hexagon	6		
Octagon	8		
Nonagon	9		
Decagon	10		
Dodecagon	12		
Icosagon	20		

2 Find the exterior and interior angle sizes of a regular heptagon.

3 Two of the exterior angles of a triangle are 120° and 130°.

   a What size is the third exterior angle?

   b Write down the size of each interior angle.

   c What type of triangle is this?

4 The interior angle of a regular polygon is 170°.

   a What size is each exterior angle?

   b How many sides has this polygon?

5 Polly calculates the exterior angle of a regular polygon as 35°. Is Polly's answer correct? Give a reason for your answer.

Activity Sheet 2.4

Activity 2.4

Drawing a circle can be helpful when constructing regular polygons. To construct a regular hexagon, draw a circle and clearly mark its centre as in **a**.

Now divide the circle into six equal sectors as shown in diagram **b**. The centre angle is 360° ÷ 6 giving 60° in each sector.

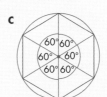

Finally join the ends of the radii as shown in diagram **c**. A regular hexagon is made up of six triangles.

Discussion 2.5

Are the triangles in the regular hexagon in the information box congruent? What type of triangles are they?

What size would the centre angles need to be to draw a regular octagon inside a circle? How many triangles would you need? What type of triangles would these be? Can the triangles be scalene for a regular polygon drawn inside a circle? Explain your answer.

Activity 2.5

Activity
Sheet 2.5

Activity 2.6

Activity
Sheet 2.6

Discussion 2.6

What does tessellation mean? Where would you see tessellating patterns? What shapes are tessellating in the picture on the left?

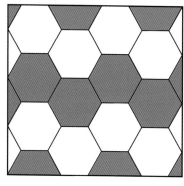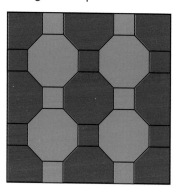

What shapes are shown in the tessellating pattern on the right? This is a **semi regular** tessellation (a tessellation of more than one type of regular polygon).

Activity 2.7

Activity
Sheet 2.7

Activity 2.8

Activity
Sheet 2.8

Discussion 2.7

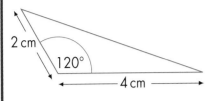

Sometimes it is necessary to construct accurate drawings. Explain the steps needed to accurately construct this triangle with a ruler and a protractor.

In this construction you have been given two sides and the included angle. What is meant by an included angle?

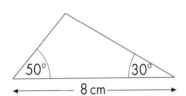

Explain how to construct this triangle with a ruler and protractor only.

What size should the missing angle be?

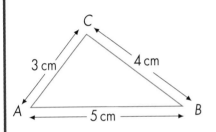

Try to explain how to construct this triangle with a ruler and pair of compasses only.

Finally, try to explain how to construct a triangle given two sides and an angle not between them as shown.

In each of the triangles, how many pieces of information were you given?

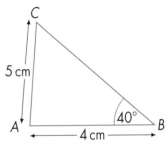

Exercise 2d

1 a Use a ruler and pair of compasses to accurately draw the triangle.

   b Measure the interior angles and find the angle sum. Check your answers with a friend.

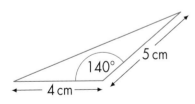

2 Construct this triangle using a ruler and protractor.

3 a Construct the following triangle.

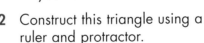

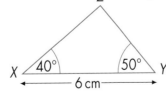

   b Measure angle *XZY* and write down your answer.

   c Measure and write down the length of *XZ* to the nearest mm.

   d Measure and write down the length of *ZY* to the nearest mm.

4 Is it possible to construct a triangle with sides of 15 cm, 6 cm and 7 cm? Give reasons for your answer.

5 **a** Construct an equilateral triangle of side 6 cm.

  b Construct a right angled triangle with side lengths 4.5 cm, 6 cm and 7.5 cm.

  c **i** Construct an isosceles triangle *ABC* where *BC* = 42 mm and *AB* = *AC*. The equal angles each measure 46°. [Hint: draw a rough sketch first to help you see the shape of the triangle.]

   ii What length is *AB*?

  d Construct a scalene triangle with sides 9 cm, 4 cm and 7 cm.

  e Construct an obtuse angled scalene triangle *ABC* with *AB* = 6 cm, ∠*A* = 35° and *BC* = 8 cm.

  f Construct an obtuse angled scalene triangle *ABC* with *AB* = 55 mm, ∠*B* = 120° and *BC* = 82 mm.

6 Construct the isosceles trapezium shown.

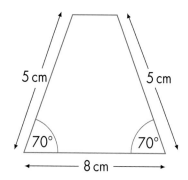

To bisect an angle means to cut it in half. This is easy to do with a pair of compasses.

Draw any angle *ABC*.

From centre *B* draw an arc (it doesn't matter what radius you choose) through *AB* and *BC*, cutting the arms of the angle at *X* and *Y*.

From centre *X*, draw an arc between the arms. Keep the radius the same and draw an arc between the arms from *Y*. The arcs intersect at *Z*.

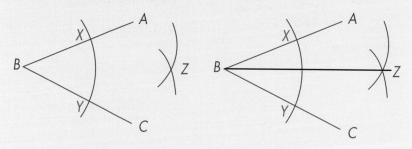

Rule a straight line from *B* to *Z*. The line *BZ* bisects angle *ABC*.

It is easy to construct an angle of 60° using a pair of compasses and a ruler.

Rule a line AB. With centre A and any radius draw an arc which cuts AB at C.

Keep the same radius and draw a second arc from C which cuts the first one at D.

Join AD and angle CAD will be 60°.

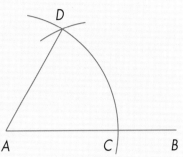

Discussion 2.8

What does perpendicular mean? What is a bisector? What, then, is a perpendicular bisector? Imagine a boat charting a course through the rocks P and Q. The captain wishes to remain the same distance from rock P as rock Q at all times. How is this possible?

P.   .Q

To construct the perpendicular bisector of two points P and Q, join the points with a straight line.

P •————————• Q

Set the radius of your pair of compasses to **more** than half the length of PQ. Draw two arcs, centred on P above and below the line.

Repeat this procedure by drawing arcs with the same radius, centred on Q above and below the line.

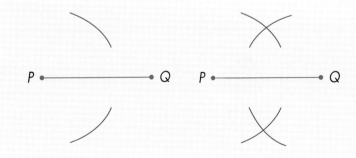

Now rule a line between the intersection points of the two sets of arcs.

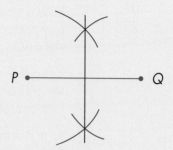

This is the perpendicular bisector of line *PQ*. Every point on this perpendicular bisector is **equidistant** from points *P* and *Q*.

Exercise 2e

SUS2e

1 Draw an acute angle and bisect it. Use a protractor to check your answer.

2 Draw an obtuse angle and bisect it.

3 Draw a reflex angle and bisect it.

4 Draw a pair of intersecting lines like those shown. Bisect all four angles using the fewest arcs and lines.

5 Construct an angle of 60°, then bisect it.

6 Look back at the first information box on page 19. If *C* were joined to *D*, what type of triangle would *ACD* be?

7 Draw a horizontal line 12 cm long and construct its perpendicular bisector.

8 A mobile phone mast is to be located between two villages 40 km apart. The phone mast must be equidistant from each village. They are shown on a scale drawing on SUS2e. On SUS2e, show the possible locations for the phone mast.

Activity Sheet 2.9

Activity 2.9

Consolidation Exercise

1 Calculate the size of the unknown angles in these polygons.

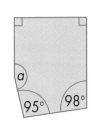
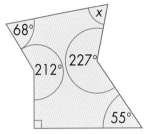

2 a How many sides has a regular polygon with an interior angle sum of 4500°?

b Find the size of each interior angle in a regular polygon with 80 sides.

3 What is the relationship between the interior and exterior angles of a polygon?

4 How many sides has a regular polygon with an interior angle of size

a 140°? **b** 156°?

5 The bases of the glasses are in the shape of regular polygons.

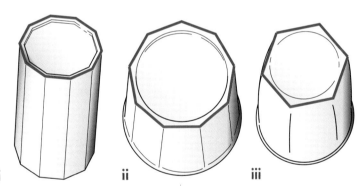

i   ii   iii

a Name each of the polygons.

b Which glass has the largest interior angle? What size is it?

c Which glass has the smallest exterior angle? What size is it?

d What can you say about the size of the interior angle of a regular polygon as the number of sides increases?

e What can you say about the size of the exterior angle of a regular polygon as the number of sides increases?

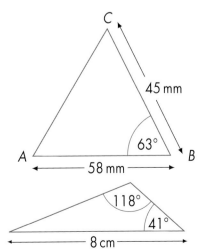

6 a Construct triangle *ABC* on the left.

b How long is *AC*?

7 Construct this triangle.

8 Draw an angle of 135° and bisect it.

3 Averages

In this chapter, I am learning to:

● calculate the mean, median and mode of a data set
● decide which average is best to use
● calculate the mean of a grouped frequency distribution.

Discussion 3.1

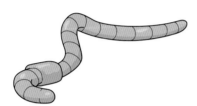

Niamh is investigating earthworms for her biology assignment. She collects 15 earthworms and measures their lengths to the nearest millimetre. Her results (in centimetres) are shown.

6.7 8.9 11.2 5.8 6.2 9.1 10.3 7.8 7.4 6.3
5.2 8.3 7.5 4.8 9.6

Niamh needs to find the **mean** length of the 15 worms. How will she calculate the mean?

Finding the mean of a data set is one way to express the average value for that data set.

To calculate the mean, add all the values together and divide the total by the number of values.

This could be written as:

$$\text{mean} = \frac{\text{total of all values}}{\text{number of values}}$$

Exercise 3a

1 Find the mean of these data sets. Round your answer to 1 decimal place where appropriate.

a 8 9 7 11 6 7

b 17 23 19 18 21 16

c 6.8 7.2 5.1 5.7

d 150 149 151 146 149 147 148 150

2   The table shows the average 24 hour temperature at Aldergrove, Northern Ireland for each month. The average for each month has been worked out using data from the years between 1834 and 1990.

Jan	Feb	Mar	April	May	June	July	Aug	Sept	Oct	Nov	Dec
4.1	4.4	5.6	7.7	10.5	13.4	14.7	14.4	12.5	9.4	6.2	4.7

Find the overall mean temperature at Aldergrove between 1834 and 1990.

The **median** is another way to find an average value.

To find the median, the values must be in order of size. The median is then the middle value.

Example 3.1

Niamh wants to find the median length of the 15 earthworms from Discussion 3.1.

To find the median she needs to arrange the lengths in order of size first.

4.8   5.2   5.8   6.2   6.3   6.7   7.4   7.5   7.8   8.3
8.9   9.1   9.6   10.3   11.2

Then Niamh picks out the middle value. Since there are 15 values, the middle value is the eighth value, which is 7.5.

The median length of the earthworms is 7.5 cm

In this case, half of the earthworms are shorter than 7.5 cm and half are longer than 7.5 cm.

Exercise 3b

1   The times taken for seven pupils to complete an ICT task are given in the table.

Pupil	Lesley	Matthew	Kevin	Rory	Sophie	Alastair	Mark
Time (minutes)	16	23	17	29	11	14	20

Find the median time taken to complete the task.

2 William arrives at the bus stop every morning at 8.00 a.m. He records how long he waits for the bus to arrive every morning for a working week.

Day	Monday	Tuesday	Wednesday	Thursday	Friday
Time for bus to arrive (minutes)	3	8	4	2	11

Find the median time that William had to wait for the bus.

3 A traffic survey records how many vehicles pass a certain place on the road between 7.30 a.m. and 8.30 a.m. every day for one week. The results are in the table.

Day	Monday	Tuesday	Wednesday	Thursday	Friday	Saturday	Sunday
Number of vehicles	652	673	1138	675	594	472	290

a On one of these days, there was a large exhibition at a nearby centre. Which day do you think this was?

b Find the median number of vehicles for this week.

c i On which days was the number of vehicles larger than the median?

ii On which days was the number of vehicles smaller than the median?

4 The price of a 2-litre container of milk in five different supermarkets is shown in the table.

Supermarket	Pricewell	Harrison's	Freshco	Carr's	Aldo's
Price	£1.28	£1.30	£1.28	£1.31	£1.30

Find the median price for two litres of milk.

If there is an even number of values, there will be two middle values. The median is the mean of these two values.

Example 3.2

The table shows the rainfall in mm for each month at Hillsborough, County Down.

Month	Jan	Feb	Mar	Apr	May	June	July	Aug	Sept	Oct	Nov	Dec
Rainfall (mm)	86	57	68	53	59	62	64	77	83	88	76	76

Find the median rainfall.

First, put the values in order.

53 57 59 62 64 68 76 76 77 83 86 88

There are two middle values, 68 and 76.

Add these together and divide by 2.

68 + 76 = 144   144 ÷ 2 = 72

The median rainfall is 72 mm.

Exercise 3c

1 Rick is doing an experiment for his chemistry GCSE. He measures the time taken for a chemical reaction to take place. He repeats the experiment four times and records the results in seconds.

   38   42   31   37

Find the median time for the chemical reaction.

2 Alison keeps a record of how much she spends on groceries every week. In the previous six weeks, the amounts were:

£67.58   £72.45   £69.80   £74.32   £64.29   £65.82.

Find the median amount that Alison spent on groceries.

3 The lengths of eight newborn babies in a maternity ward were:

51 cm 48 cm 45 cm 49 cm 54 cm 46 cm 50 cm 44 cm.

Find the median length of these babies.

The **mode** is another commonly used average value.

The mode is the value that occurs most often.

There can be no mode (all the values occur the same number of times).

There can be more than one mode (two or more values occur most often).

Finding the modal value is the same as finding the mode.

Example 3.3

A form tutor records how many days each pupil in his class was absent in the month of September.

   0 3 1 0 1 0 0 0 0 6 3 0
      1 2 0 0 2 0 1 0 0 0

The mode of the data set is 0 since there are more 0s than any other value.

Exercise 3d

1 Find the mode for each of these data sets.

a 13 14 13 14 14 12 15

b 100 105 109 106 100 105 107 105

c 9.8 9.7 9.8 9.9 9.8 9.6 9.9 9.2 9.5 9.9

d 0 1 0 −1 −1 0 1 1 −1

e 5 5 5 5 5 5 5 5 5

2 Pupils may borrow up to five CDs at a time from the school library. Sophie asks 12 of her classmates how many CDs they have from the school library at that time. The answers are given.

4 2 0 1 0 5 3 0 2 5 4

Find the modal number of CDs borrowed by Sophie's classmates.

3 The boot sizes of the boys in a football team are:

7 6 $8\frac{1}{2}$ 9 7 6 7 $6\frac{1}{2}$ 8 $7\frac{1}{2}$ 7

What is the modal boot size?

4 During a six-week ICT course, Aidan records how many mistakes he makes in the weekly word processing test.

Week	1	2	3	4	5	6
Number of mistakes	3	2	1	3	2	3

What is the modal number of mistakes that Aidan made?

Discussion 3.2

Claudia is hoping to grow courgettes. She takes 10 pots and plants five seeds in each pot.

The numbers of seeds which germinated (started to grow) in each pot are shown.

3 4 3 2 0 2 3 4 4 4

Claudia says that the average number of seeds to germinate was 4.

Her friend Josef says that the average number of seeds to germinate was 3.

Which average (mean, median or mode) was Claudia using?

Which average (mean, median or mode) was Josef using?

The seed company carried out a larger survey using 100 pots each with five seeds. The mean, median and mode were calculated. The results are shown.

Mean = 3.7   Median = 4   Mode = 3 and 4

Which of the three averages would be most useful for the seed company to use for advertising these seeds?

Exercise 3e

1 The salaries of six office workers are shown.

| £22 500 | £17 425 | £22 500 |
| £14 650 | £18 950 | £14 250 |

a Find the mean salary for these workers.

b Find the modal salary.

c Find the median salary.

d The manager of the company wants to advertise for a new assistant. He wants to include the average salary in his job advertisement. Which average should he use? Do you think this is fair?

2 In a competition 17 basketball players were each given 30 shots at the basket. The mean number of baskets scored was 25 and the median number was 19.

a How many players scored more than 19 baskets?

b How many players scored fewer than 19 baskets?

c Each of the statements below is either true, false or there it is not enough information to say. Copy the statements and write T (true), F (false) or N (not enough information) after each one.

Give a reason for your answer each time.

i At least one player scored 19 baskets.

ii At least one player scored 25 baskets.

iii One player scored 30 baskets.

iv The total number of shots taken altogether by all the players was 510.

v The total number of baskets scored altogether by all the players was 435.

3 An estate agent has five houses for sale on Sunny Street. They are priced as follows:

House number	23	48	51	64	67
Price	£269 000	£185 000	£267 000	£263 500	£268 500

a Calculate the mean house price.

b What is the median house price?

c Why do you think there is a large difference between the mean house price and the median house price?

d The estate agent wants to use an average value for houses on Sunny Street. Do you think the mean or the median house price is more typical for Sunny Street? Give a reason for your answer.

e Explain why the mode would not be suitable.

**Activity
Sheet 3.1**

Activity 3.1

Discussion 3.3

Number of goals scored	Number of matches
0	4
1	6
2	3
3	1
4	0
5	1

Hannah and Emily have been given the table showing the number of goals scored by their hockey team during last season.

They want to find the mean number of goals scored per match.

Emily writes the data out like this:

0 0 0 0 1 1 1 1 1 1 2 2 2 3 5

Discuss, with a partner, what Emily has done.

Emily adds all these values together and gets 20. She then calculates 20 ÷ 15 to get 1.33333333333.

Emily says that the mean number of goals scored is 1.3 to 1 decimal place (d.p.)

Why did Emily divide by 15?

Hannah says that there is a quicker way to calculate the mean by multiplying the number of goals by number of matches. She puts the answers to her multiplication calculations in a new column in the table. She then finds the total of this column and divides by the total number of matches.

Her method is shown.

Number of goals scored	Number of matches	Number of goals × number of matches
0	4	0
1	6	6
2	3	6
3	1	3
4	0	0
5	1	5
		Total = 20

20 ÷ 15 = 1.33333333333

Mean number of goals = 1.3 to 1 d.p.

Why do you think Hannah's method works for finding the mean?

The table shows the number of goals scored by a different hockey team during last season. Work with a partner to copy and complete this table to find the mean number of goals scored by this hockey team.

Number of goals scored	Number of matches	Number of goals × number of matches
0	2	
1	7	
2	2	
3	2	
4	1	
5	1	

What is the mean number of goals? Which method did you use?

Exercise 3f

Number in household	Number of pupils
2	1
3	4
4	8
5	6
6	0
7	1

Number of flowers	Number of pots
0	1
1	0
2	3
3	3
4	7
5	11

1 Ryan carries out a survey to find out the size of households of the pupils in his class. He puts the information in a table.

a How many pupils are there in Ryan's class?

b Copy the table and include an extra column as shown in Discussion 3.3.

c Use your table to find the mean number of people per household.

2 Thirty visitors to Belfast were asked if they had been to the Giant's Causeway and, if so, how many times they had been there before. The results are shown in the table.

Number of visits to the Giant's Causeway	Number of people
0	4
1	12
2	8
3	4
4	2

Find the mean number of visits per visitor.

3 To test a new variety of tulip, 25 plant pots are planted with five tulip bulbs each. The number of flowers in each pot is noted on a certain day. The table shows the results.

Find the mean number of flowers per pot.

Number letters in word	Number of words
1	4
2	7
3	11
4	21
5	10
6	5
7	3
8	2

4 Clare takes the novel she is reading and opens it randomly. She counts the number of words on one page which have one letter, two letters, three letters, etc. She puts her results in a table.

a How many letters are there in the longest word on that page in Clare's book?

b How many words are there on that page?

c Calculate the mean number of letters per word.

Cups of coffee	Office workers
0	8
1	11
2	14
3	5
4	0
5	2

5 In an effort to improve catering services, some office workers were asked how many cups of coffee they had bought from the coffee machine the day before. The results are shown in the table.

a How many office workers took part in the survey?

b How many cups of coffee were bought from the machine altogether on that day?

c Calculate the mean number of cups of coffee bought per office worker.

Discussion 3.4

Amount spent (in £s)	Number of customers
1–20	7
21–40	11
41–60	12
61–80	8
81–100	1
101–120	1

The manager of a supermarket carries out a survey about customer spending. The amount (to the nearest £) spent by 40 customers is recorded and the results are summarised in the table.

What was the largest amount spent?

What was the smallest amount spent?

A customer spent £60.59. In which group in the table would this amount be counted?

How you could adapt the method used in the last exercise to find an estimate of the mean amount spent? Why is this an **estimate** of the mean?

Height (h) in centimetres	Number of pupils
$150 \leqslant h < 155$	2
$155 \leqslant h < 160$	5
$160 \leqslant h < 165$	9
$165 \leqslant h < 170$	7
$170 \leqslant h < 175$	4
$175 \leqslant h < 180$	2
$180 \leqslant h < 185$	1

The table shows the heights of 30 Year 12 pupils.

What do you think $\leqslant$ means?

A pupil is 167 cm tall. In which group in the table would this pupil be counted?

What about a pupil who is 170 cm tall?

Example 3.4

To find the mean height of the pupils, a middle value (mid-point) can be used to represent each group. Set up a new table with two extra columns – one for the middle value for each group and one for the middle values multiplied by the number of pupils in that group.

Height (h) in centimetres	Mid-point (x)	Number of pupils (f)	Frequency × mid-point (fx)
$150 \leqslant h < 155$	152.5	2	305
$155 \leqslant h < 160$	157.5	5	787.5
$160 \leqslant h < 165$	162.5	9	1462.5
$165 \leqslant h < 170$	167.5	7	1172.5
$170 \leqslant h < 175$	172.5	4	690
$175 \leqslant h < 180$	177.5	2	355
$180 \leqslant h < 185$	182.5	1	182.5
		Total number of pupils (Σf) = 30	Total of frequency × mid-point (Σfx) = 4955

It is usual to use 'x' for the mid-points and 'f' for number of pupils (frequency).

We can use a formula to work out the mean:

$$\text{mean} = \frac{\text{sum of (frequency} \times \text{mid-points)}}{\text{total frequency}}$$

We can write this using symbols:

$$\text{mean} = \frac{\Sigma fx}{\Sigma f}$$

mean = 4955 ÷ 30 = 165.2

The mean height of the 30 pupils is 165.2 cm.

Exercise 3g

In this exercise, give your answer to 1 decimal place where appropriate.

1 Use the data in the table from Discussion 3.4 on supermarket spending for this question. Calculate an estimate of the mean amount spent by the 40 customers.

2 Twenty teachers were asked how long it had taken them to get to work that morning. Copy and complete the table and calculate an estimate of the mean time taken to get to work.

Time (t) in minutes	Mid-point (x)	Number of teachers	fx
$0 \leqslant t < 10$	5	1	5
$10 \leqslant t < 20$	15	4	60
$20 \leqslant t < 30$		8	
$30 \leqslant t < 40$		5	
$40 \leqslant t < 50$		1	
$50 \leqslant t < 60$		1	
		Total frequency =	Total time =

3 For her statistics assignment, Phillipa asked 30 Year 10 pupils how much they had spent in the tuckshop that lunchtime. She recorded her results in a table. She uses the letter a to represent the amount spent.

Amount spent (a) in pence	Mid-point (x)	Number of pupils	fx
$0 \leqslant a < 0.50$		8	
$0.50 \leqslant a < 1.00$		11	
$1.00 \leqslant a < 1.50$		7	
$1.50 \leqslant a < 2.00$		2	
$2.00 \leqslant a < 2.50$		1	
$2.50 \leqslant a < 3.00$		1	
		Total frequency =	Total amount spent =

Copy and complete the table and calculate an estimate of the mean amount spent.

4 Alex is doing a survey on how the pupils in his class spend their free time. He asks each pupil how long they spent using the internet the previous day and records the results in a table.

Time (t) in minutes	Mid-point (x)	Number of pupils	fx
0 ⩽ t < 20	10	2	20
20 ⩽ t < 40	30	5	
40 ⩽ t < 60		12	
60 ⩽ t < 80		2	
80 ⩽ t < 100		0	
100 ⩽ t < 120		1	
		Total frequency =	Total time =

Copy and complete the table and calculate an estimate of the mean time spent using the internet.

5   The times taken for 100 runners to complete a 5-kilometre fun run are recorded in the table.

Time taken (t) in minutes	11 ⩽ t < 15	15 ⩽ t < 20	20 ⩽ t < 25	25 ⩽ t < 30	30 ⩽ t < 40
Number of runners	23	28	29	12	8

a Put this information in a table that is suitable for calculating an estimate of the mean.

b Calculate an estimate of the mean time taken to complete the 5-kilometre run.

6   Fifty householders living in the same street were asked how much their electricity bill was for the previous quarter. The results are summarised in the table.

Electricity bill (b) for last quarter (£s)	Frequency
0 ⩽ b < 50	2
50 ⩽ b < 100	6
100 ⩽ b < 150	11
150 ⩽ b < 200	23
200 ⩽ b < 250	6
250 ⩽ b < 300	2

a How many householders had an electricity bill less than £200?

b Put the information in a table that is suitable for calculating an estimate of the mean.

c Calculate an estimate of the mean for the electricity bills.

**Activity
Sheet 3.2**

Activity 3.2

Consolidation Exercise

1 The manager of a gaelic football team ordered new boots for his squad. The sizes of the boots he ordered were:

10 9 10 11 8 10 9 11 10 10 9 12

9 9 10 9 11 10

a What was the modal size of boots ordered?

b Find the median size of boots.

c Calculate the mean boot size.

2 Rory asks some pupils in Year 10 how many books they borrowed from the school library that term. He puts the results of his survey in a table.

Number of books borrowed	0	1	2	3	4	5	6	7	8
Number of pupils	3	5	7	10	5	3	6	2	1

a How many pupils took part in the survey?

b What was the modal number of books borrowed?

c How many books were borrowed altogether by the pupils in the survey?

d Calculate the mean number of books borrowed.

3 As part of a tourist survey, visitors to a Folk Museum were asked how far they had travelled to get to the museum. The answers are summarised in the table.

Distance travelled (d miles)	Number of people
$0 \leqslant d < 20$	11
$20 \leqslant d < 40$	17
$40 \leqslant d < 60$	28
$60 \leqslant d < 80$	42
$80 \leqslant d < 100$	35
$100 \leqslant d < 120$	3

a How many visitors took part in the survey?

b Calculate an estimate of the mean number of miles travelled by these visitors.

4 Expressions, formulae and equations

In this chapter, I am learning to:

- expand brackets
- factorise expressions
- construct and use formulae
- simplify expressions
- solve equations.

Discussion 4.1

Lewis is looking at his older sister's Maths homework. She has got all of question 1 right!

a $2(x + 4) = 2x + 8$ ✓   b $4(y - 3) = 4y - 12$ ✓

c $3(5 + 2m) = 15 + 6m$ ✓   d $6(2q - 5) = 12q - 30$ ✓

Lewis says, 'I haven't done this topic yet but I think I know why the answers are correct'.

Look at each of the questions and work out why the answers are correct.

Work with a partner to expand the brackets for each expression:

a $4(g - 3)$ b $10(2m + 5n)$ c $6(5 - 4d)$

When we write an expression such as $2(3x - 4)$ as $6x - 8$, we have **expanded the brackets.** To expand brackets, we multiply everything inside the bracket by the number or term immediately in front of it.

Exercise 4a

Copy and rewrite these expressions by expanding the brackets.

1   $5(f + 7)$ 6 $4(6e - 3f)$

2   $3(m - 7)$ 7 $6(5t - 4)$

3   $2(3h + 4)$ 8 $100(5t - 2)$

4   $10(9 - 7k)$ 9 $3(3m - 3n)$

5   $8(2g + 3h)$ 10 $0(6h + 54)$

Discussion 4.2

The term outside the bracket is not always a number.

Lewis looks at question 2 from his sister's homework.

a $t(5-q) = 5t - tq$ ✓   b $4j(2k-4) = 8jk - 16j$ ✓

c $2p(6-q) = 12p - 2pq$ ✓   d $3f(5g+5) = 15fg + 15f$ ✓

e $d(6-d) = 6d - d^2$ ✓   f $2k(3j + 5k - 2) = 6jk + 10k^2 - 4k$ ✓

Explain how the correct answer was obtained for each of the questions.

Work with a partner to expand the brackets in these expressions:

a $w(v + 7)$ b $2g(5 - 3h)$

c $2m(3 - m)$ d $3v(5v + 2w - 4)$

Exercise 4b

Expand the brackets in these expressions.

1 $a(3b - 7)$ 6 $4x(2x + y)$

2 $5m(2 - 6n)$ 7 $10t(2v - t)$

3 $3p(q + 7)$ 8 $6e(2e - 5f + 2)$

4 $g(g + 2h)$ 9 $b(2c - 3b + d)$

5 $3c(4 + c)$ 10 $e^2(2f + g)$

Discussion 4.3

Look at the function machine.

What expression would complete the last line of this function machine?

$5(2m - 4)$
$3(7 + q)$
?

$10m - 20$
$21 + 3q$
$9 + 6y$

'Undoing' expanding brackets is called **factorising**.

To factorise an expression, look at all the terms in the expression and find the largest number that divides into all of the terms. This number will go outside the bracket. Then work out the expression that goes inside the bracket by dividing.

Example 4.1

a Factorise $12q - 6p$. **b** Factorise fully $3p + 6pq$.

a 6 is the largest number that divides into both $12q$ and $6p$ so it goes outside the bracket.

$2q - p$ goes into the bracket (divide 6 into $12q$ and $6p$) so the solution is $6(2q - p)$.

You can check your answer by expanding the brackets.

If you do not find the largest number that divides into both $12q$ and $3p$, you have not factorised fully. For example $3(4q - 2p)$ is not a fully factorised answer. Why not?

b In this expression there is a number and a variable that can be divided into both $3p$ and $6pq$ so we can take $3p$ outside the brackets. The solution is $3p(1 + 2q)$. This is because $3p + 6pq$ divided by $3p$ gives $1 + 2q$ and this expression goes into the brackets. If we had only taken 3 or p outside the brackets we would not have factorised fully; we must take $3p$ outside.

Exercise 4c

Factorise the following expressions fully.

1 $15m - 5n$	**9** $48 - 16x - 32y$
2 $24 + 16f$	**10** $12u + 42v + 27w$
3 $20t - 4v$	**11** $12k + 4ak$
4 $10 - 25y$	**12** $6pq - 2q$
5 $6d + 18e - 3f$	**13** $9mn + 21n$
6 $8t^2 + 12$	**14** $5fg + 15g - 10$
7 $18y - 45$	**15** $8t - tw + 7t^2$
8 $35k - 25j + 15$	**16** $2x^2 + 4x$

Expressions can be **simplified** by adding **like terms**.

The expression $11 + 5t^2 + 3v - t^2 + 6v - 8$ has three different types of terms: terms in t^2, terms in v and numbers.

Example 4.2

Simplify this expression: $11 + 5t^2 + 3v - t^2 + 6v - 8$.

First, rearrange the expression so that like terms are beside each other.

$11 - 8 + 5t^2 - t^2 + 3v + 6v$

Remember to include the sign when you are rearranging. The last term in this expression is –8, not 8 so you must move the minus sign along with the 8.

Now add the like terms ($11 - 8 = 3$, $5t^2 - t^2 = 4t^2$, and $3v + 6v = 9v$) so the answer is:

$3 + 4t^2 + 9v$.

Discussion 4.4

Clare and Simon have been given this question to answer:

Expand the brackets and simplify this expression.
$5(3j - 2) - 2(4j + 1)$

Look at Clare and Simon's working.

Clare's work:

$5(3j - 2) - 2(4j + 1) = 15j - 10 - 8j - 2$
$= 15j - 8j - 10 - 2$
$= 7j - 12$

Simon's work:

$5(3j - 2) - 2(4j + 1) = 15j - 10 - 8j + 2$
$= 15j - 8j - 10 + 2$
$= 7j - 8$

One of these is correct. Can you see who made a mistake and where it is in the working?

Exercise 4d

1 Simplify these expressions.

a $4e + 7f - e + 6f$

b $9u + 2v - v + 7 - 5v + 2u$

c $5 - 2m + 7 - 8n - 3m + 11n$

d $i^2 + i^2 + 7 - 3j + 3i^2 - 10$

e $8x^2 - 4x + 7 + 3x^2 - 2x - 14$

f $4pq - 8 - 7pq + pq + 11$

g $5ab - b^2 + 9ab - 5b^2 - ba$

h $10a^2b + 5ab + 3a^2b + 2ab + 4ab^2$

2 Expand the brackets and simplify these expressions.

a $4(2c + 3) + 3(5c + 2)$ b $6 + 2(3x - 7)$

c $5(7v - 1) + 2(v - 3)$ d $a(3b - 1) + b(3a - 1)$

e $4(6 - 2x) - 2(2 - x)$ f $d(d - 4) + 5d^2$

g $3(2t - 3) + 5(2t - 4)$ h $5mn - m(2n + 7) + 3m$

Activity Sheet 4.1

Activity 4.1

$3x + 2 = 17$ is an **equation**. It has an equals sign whereas an expression does not. We can **solve** this equation to find the value of x.

Discussion 4.5

Connor and Margaret are solving the equation $3x + 2 = 17$.

They both get the correct answer but their working out looks different.

Connor's method:

$3x + 2 = 17$

$3x + 2 - 2 = 17 - 2$

$3x = 15$

$x = 15 \div 3$

$x = 5$

Margaret's method:

$3x + 2 = 17$

$3x = 17 - 2$

$3x = 15$

$x = 15 \div 3$

$x = 5$

Discuss, with a partner, what is the same and what is different about the two methods.

Exercise 4e

Solve these equations.

1   $2m + 4 = 14$

2   $3t - 7 = 11$

3   $3q - 1 = 14$

4   $5g - 3 = 32$

5   $10 - j = 6$

6   $14 = 2f - 14$

7   $2e + 1 = 17$

8   $\frac{d}{12} = 3$

9   $\frac{n}{3} + 1 = 6$

10   $\frac{2m}{3} + 4 = 12$

11   $\frac{3x}{4} - 1 = 2$

12   $\frac{4n}{5} - 3 = 5$

Example 4.3

Solve the equation:

$7x + 2 = 20 - 2x$

You can solve this equation by collecting the xs to the left hand side of the equals sign and the numbers to the right hand side.

$7x + 2 - 2 = 20 - 2x - 2$ [−2 from each side of the equation]

$7x = 18 - 2x$

$7x + 2x = 18 - 2x + 2x$ [+2x to each side of the equation]

$9x = 18$ [now simplify by dividing each side by 9]

$x = 2$

Discussion 4.6

Describe how to solve $3x + 5 = 6x - 10$. You must state all steps clearly. Is there more than one possible method?

Exercise 4f

Solve these equations, showing each stage of your working.

1   $6t = 4t - 10$

2   $8m = 20 - 2m$

3   $7q = 42 - 7q$

4   $4x + 7 = 3x + 10$

5   $5t - 4 = 16 + t$

6   $2d + 7 = 12 - 3d$

7   $7v - 8 = 12 - 3v$

8   $10 - 3q = 5q + 14$

9   $7t + 5 = 5t + 10$

10   $7d + 6 = 9 - 3d$

Example 4.4

Solve the equation:

$$5(2x + 4) = 32.$$

$$10x + 20 = 32 \qquad \text{[first expand the brackets]}$$

$$10x + 20 - 20 = 32 - 20 \qquad \text{[subtract 20 from both sides of the equation]}$$

$$10x = 12 \qquad \text{[divide both sides by 10]}$$

$$x = 1.2$$

Exercise 4g

Solve these equations, showing each stage of your working.

1 $18 = 2(x + 3)$
2 $2(2x - 7) = 12$
3 $5(2m - 4) = 12$
4 $10 + 3(h - 4) = 4$
5 $3(2x - 1) - 1 = 20$

6 $2(3x + 5) = 4(x + 5)$
7 $3(2x + 1) = 4(x + 1)$
8 $3(m - 6) = 5(2m + 2)$
9 $2 + 3(2m + 1) = 8m$
10 $3(4p - 1) = 5(2p - 4) + 12$

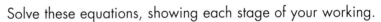

Discussion 4.7

Discuss, with a partner, how you could use inverse operations to solve the equation.

$$\frac{3g + 2}{5} = 7$$

Share your method with the class. Discuss the differences and similarities in the methods used.

Exercise 4h

Solve these equations, showing each stage of your working.

1 $\dfrac{g - 2}{4} = 2$
2 $\dfrac{3k + 6}{3} = 4$
3 $\dfrac{3i - 1}{5} = 4$

4 $\dfrac{2t + 5}{5} = 10$
5 $\dfrac{3y + 9}{3} = 2$
6 $\dfrac{2k + 3}{2} = 4$

7 $\dfrac{2d - 3}{2} = 2$
8 $\dfrac{3(2d - 11)}{11} = 3$

Activity Sheet 4.2

Activity 4.2

A **formula** is a rule connecting two or more **variables**.

For example, in the formula

$y = 3x - 2$

y and x are variables because they can take different values. If we know the value of x, we can use the formula to find the value of y.

Example 4.5

Use the formula $y = 3x - 2$ to find the value of y when

a $x = 5$ **b** $x = -4$.

a Substitute 5 into the formula instead of x.

$y = 3 \times 5 - 2$

$y = 15 - 2$

$y = 13$

b Substitute -4 into the formula instead of x.

$y = 3 \times -4 - 2$

$y = -12 - 2$

$y = -14$

Exercise 4i

1 Use the formula $c = 4d + 1$ to find c when:

   a $d = 2$ **b** $d = 10$ **c** $d = -2$.

2 Use the formula $y = 5x - 8$ to find y when:

   a $x = 4$ **b** $x = 1$ **c** $x = -6$.

3 Use the formula $v = u + 10t$ to find v when:

   a $u = 2$ and $t = 3$ **b** $u = 0$ and $t = 6$ **c** $u = -20$ and $t = 2$.

4 Use the formula $s = t^2 + 1$ to find s when:

   a $t = 3$ **b** $t = 0$ **c** $t = 12$.

5 Use the formula $y = x^2 - 3x$ to find y when:

   a $x = 5$ **b** $x = 2$ **c** $x = 0$ **d** $x = -2$.

6 Use the formula $F = ma$ to find F when:

   a $m = 3.5$ and $a = 10$ **b** $m = 3.5$ and $a = -10$

   c $m = 8$ and $a = -2.5$.

Example 4.6

A taxi firm charges £3 for each journey plus 5p for every minute of the journey.

a Write a formula for the cost of any journey.

Use C for the cost in £s and m for the number of minutes.

b Use your formula to work out the cost of a journey lasting 18 minutes.

c A journey costs £4.25. How many minutes did this journey take?

a Write the formula in words (or just say it to yourself).

Cost equals £3 plus 5p times the number of minutes.

Then write this using algebra.

$C = 3 + 0.05m$

Remember that both amounts of money must be in £s for the formula to work.

b $C = 3 + 0.05 \times 18$

$\quad = 3 + 0.90 = 3.90$

Cost = £3.90

c First substitute for C = £4.25 and then solve the equation to find m.

$4.25 = 3 + 0.05\,m$

$1.25 = 0.05\,m$

$m = \dfrac{1.25}{0.05} = 25$ so the journey time is 25 minutes

Exercise 4j

1 Cheryl has a summer job picking strawberries on a fruit farm. She is paid £20 per day plus 30p for every kilogram of strawberries that she picks.

a Write down a formula for the amount Cheryl gets paid for a day's work.

Use P for the amount she gets paid in £s and k for the number of kilograms of strawberries that she picks.

b One day Cheryl picks 28 kilograms of strawberries.

Use your formula to find how much she gets paid that day.

2 During the first 16 weeks of its life a baby gains around 170 grams every week.

  a Write down a formula for calculating the baby's weight at any age up to 16 weeks.

  Use W for the baby's weight in grams, b for the baby's weight at birth and n for its age in weeks.

  b Use your formula to find the weight of an 11-week-old baby who weighed 3140 grams at birth.

3 Alex buys a box of teddy bears for £83 and sells them for £3.50 each on his market stall.

  a Write down a formula for the profit Alex makes.

  Use P for the profit (in £s) and n for the number of teddy bears that Alex sells.

  b Use your formula to find Alex's profit if he sells 53 teddy bears.

  c What is Alex's profit if he sells 22 teddy bears?

  d Use your formula to find how many teddy bears Alex sold if his profit was £270.50.

4 Beth's quarterly electricity bill for her business is made up of a standing charge of £15.58 and 16 pence for each unit of electricity she uses.

  a Write down a formula to calculate Beth's total electricity bill.

  Use B for the total amount of the bill and n for the number of units of electricity used.

  b Use your formula to find Beth's electricity bill if she uses 908 units of electricity.

  c How many units of electricity has Beth used if her bill is £65.38?

Consolidation Exercise

1 Expand the brackets in these expressions. Then simplify your answer if necessary.

  a $5(h - 7)$ b $6(2v + 5) + v$

  c $12 + 5(3m - 8)$ d $2(x - 4) + 5(2y + 6) + 3y$

  e $a(b - 7)$ f $w(w - 4) + 4(2w + 1)$

  g $6(t + 3) - 3(3 - 4t)$ h $2k(3k - 4) - 5(k + 2)$

  i $a(2b - 3) + b(2a - 3)$ j $6pq + 4p(2p - 3q) - 5$

2 Use the formula $y = 3x - 5$ to find the value of y when

   a $x = 2$ **b** $x = 0$ **c** $x = -1$ **d** $x = -10$.

3 Use the formula $V = IR$ to find the value of V when

   a $I = 10$ and $R = 3$ **b** $I = 9.3$ and $R = 0$

   c $I = 1.02$ and $R = 7$

   d Find the value of I when $V = 38.27$ and $R = 4.3$.

4 Use the formula $s = t^2 + 2t$ to find the value of s when

   a $t = 5$ **b** $t = 0$ **c** $t = -1$ **d** $t = -2.5$.

5 Factorise these expressions fully.

   a $5a + 15$ **b** $8d - 24$ **c** $6t - 22v + 10$

   d $t^2 + 2t$ **e** $12q - 12$ **f** $14ab - 2b$

   g $3ab + 5bc$ **h** $2abc - 6bcd$ **i** $10p^2 + 4p$

   j $9mn + 15n^2$

6 Solve these equations.

   a $3m + 7 = 22$ **b** $5g - 10 = 3g$

   c $\frac{p}{3} = 7$ **d** $\frac{4p}{3} = 7$

   e $6(q - 1) = 12$ **f** $27 = 3(d + 4)$

   g $7h + 3 = 5h - 11$ **h** $5t - 4 = 12 - 3t$

   i $9j + 20 - 4j = j - 4$ **j** $5k - 7 = 2(k + 4)$

   k $2(w - 4) = 10$ **l** $6p + 7 = 49 - p$

5 Ratio and proportion

In this chapter, I am learning to:

- use ratio and proportion
- use and draw scale diagrams
- understand and use bearings.

Discussion 5.1

A recipe for 12 shortbread fingers uses 240 g of butter. Sinead and Tom are discussing how much butter would be needed to make 16 shortbread fingers.

Sinead says that you divide 240 by 12 and then multiply by 16.

Tom says that you multiply 240 by $\frac{4}{3}$ as $\frac{16}{12}$ can be simplified to $\frac{4}{3}$.

Which of these methods would you prefer to use? Give a reason for your answer.

Activity
Sheet 5.1

Activity 5.1

Discussion 5.2

This photograph is 8 cm wide.

Kate wants to enlarge it so that the ratio of the width of the original photograph to the width of the enlarged photograph is 1 : 2.

What would be the new width of the photograph?

Measure the height of the photograph.

What would be the new height of the photograph?

Kate also wants a copy of the photograph which is 12 cm wide.

She says that the width would be 1.5 times bigger so the ratio for this enlargement would be 1 : 1.5. Is she correct?

If the ratio 2 : 5 were used, what would the width of the enlarged photograph be?

What about the ratio 4 : 3?

Exercise 5a

1 Copy and complete the table.

	Ratio	Old measurement	New measurement	Is new measurement bigger or smaller than original?
a	1:4		12 cm	
b	2:5	15 mm		
c		6 cm	10 cm	
d	5:8		40 cm	
e		2.5 cm	3 cm	Bigger
f		22 cm	8 cm	Smaller

2 A photo measures 4 cm by 6 cm. The photo is enlarged in the ratio 4:5. What are its new dimensions?

3 Sean imports an image of the Eiffel tower into his project. The image is 10 cm high by 8 cm wide. Sean wants to resize the image so that it is 6 cm wide.

   a What ratio would he need to use for this enlargement?

   b What would be the height of the image after this enlargement?

4 A diagram measures 80 mm by 50 mm after an enlargement in the ratio 5:2. What were the original dimensions of the diagram?

5 An image is enlarged so that the length of the new image is 3.5 times the length of the old image. What is the ratio of this enlargement?

6 Niamh wants to build a scale model of the Empire State Building. The actual building is 381 metres high. She is trying to work out what ratio she could use for her model. She wants her model to be at least 90 cm tall. Her mum says that it has to fit into the cupboard under the stairs which has a height of 1.5 metres.

   a Which of the following ratios could Niamh use? (There may be more than one possible answer!) Give reasons for your answer(s).

1:3000	1:100	1:300
2:500	3:100	3:1000

   b If she uses one of these ratios, what height is the tallest model that Niamh can make?

Discussion 5.3

Kevin is looking at a plan of his house and garden. The scale on the plan says 1 : 100.

Katy says that this means that everything in real life is 100 times bigger than it is on the plan. Is she right?

On the plan, the width of their kitchen is 3.2 cm. What is the actual width of the kitchen in metres?

The garden path on the plan measures 11.5 cm. What is the actual length of the path?

Many different scales are used on maps or plans depending on the detail required.

Which of these scales would provide most detail in a scale drawing?

1 : 5   1 : 10   1 : 200   1 : 250 000

Where might each of these scales be used?

On a map a lake is 2.3 cm long. The scale of the map is 1 : 250 000. How could we find the actual length of the lake in kilometres?

Exercise 5b

1   Maps and plans are drawn using the following scales.

   1 : 50   1 : 5000   1 : 5   1 : 50000   1 : 500

   a Which of these scales would show the most detail on a map or plan?

   b Which would show least detail?

2   On a 1 : 50 000 map of the Sperrin mountains, Gortin Glen Forest is 12 cm long.

   a What is the actual length of the forest?

   b The distance between the Old Church Bridge and Owenreagh bridge is 1.9 km. How far apart will they be on the map?

3   Ryan and Sinead are planning a walk in the Mourne mountains. They are using a 1 : 25 000 map. Copy and complete the table showing the distances of the first four legs of their walk.

Leg		Distance on map (cm)	Actual distance (km)
a	Carrick Little Car Park to edge of Annalong Wood	7.1	
b	Edge of Annalong Wood to Forest corner	5.9	
c	Forest corner to Blue Lough		1.1
d	Blue Lough to Buzzard's Roost		0.7

4 Damian has walked along the River Lagan path from Shaw's Bridge to the Boat Club at Stranmillis. He measures the distance as 13.5 cm on a 1 : 12 000 map of the Belfast area.

a The path along the river is not straight. How do you think Damian measured the distance on the map?

b Find the actual distance that Damian walked.

c The distance along the path from the Boat Club to the Waterfront Hall is 3.8 cm on the map. What is the actual distance?

5 Emma is building a 1 : 15 scale model of a classic luxury car.

Copy and complete this table showing different features of the car and the model.

Feature	Measurement on car	Measurement on model (mm)
Length	608.4 cm	
Width	199 cm	
Height		1088 mm
Number of seats	4	
Wheelbase		254 mm

Discussion 5.4

The sails of the boat are triangular.

Both sails are isosceles. The smaller sail has dimensions of 2 m, 3 m and 3 m. How could you draw an accurate representation of this sail? What would be a sensible scale to use? The larger sail has dimensions of 2.5 m, 4.5 m and 4.5 m. A scale of 1 cm to 50 cm is chosen. What size will the scale drawing be? A scale of 1 cm to 50 cm can be written 1 : 50. To make accurate drawings of these sails you will need to use your knowledge of constructions from Chapter 2. Describe fully how you would construct a scale diagram for each sail.

Exercise 5c

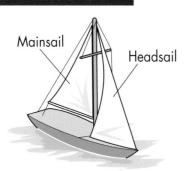

Mainsail   Headsail

1 The sloop shown has two triangular sails. The headsail is isosceles with a base of 4 m and a pair of equal angles of size 65°.

   a Construct an accurate scale drawing of the headsail using a scale of 1 : 50.

   b Measure the length of a side of the sail in the scale drawing and calculate the real length of the sail.

   c The mainsail is a right-angled scalene triangle with base 5 m and height 8 m. Use a scale of 1 : 100 and construct an accurate scale drawing of the mainsail.

   d What is the real length of the third side of this mainsail?

   e Measure the two acute angles on your scale drawing and hence write down the real angles of the sail.

2 Construct accurate scale drawings of the triangular crazy paving stones shown. Use the given scales.

   a scale 1 : 20   b scale 1 : 10   c scale 1 : 5

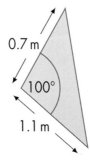

0.7 m

100°

1.1 m

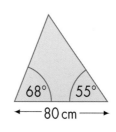

68°   55°

← 80 cm →

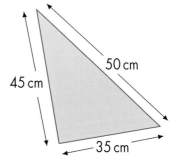

50 cm

45 cm

35 cm

3 Bill, Bob and Barry live in Belfast, Armagh and Tyrone respectively.

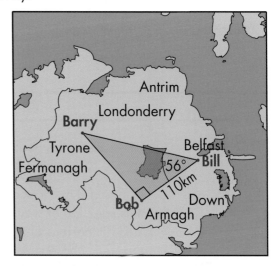

   a Write the scale of 1 cm to 10 km in the form 1 : x.

   b Draw an accurate scale drawing using the scale in part a to show the locations of the boys.

   c How far does Barry live from i Bob ii Bill as the crow flies?

4 Construct an accurate scale drawing of the rockery shown. Use a scale of 1 : 250. What is the length of the third side?

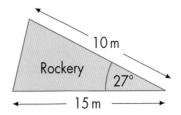

Rockery
10 m
27°
15 m

Activity Sheet 5.2

Activity 5.2

Discussion 5.5

A fishing boat out at sea wants to head back to port. The skipper has a chart (map) of the sea area and he knows the position of the boat on the map. He sees from the map that he needs to head due west to get to the port. What else does the skipper need to know so that he can turn the boat in the correct direction?

Another fishing boat that is nearby also wants to head to the port. That skipper also has a chart of the sea area and he knows the position of his boat on the map. He sees from the map that the direction he needs to travel in is somewhere between south west and west. How will he know what angle to turn his boat to head in that direction?

Bearings are used to describe the direction from one point to another.

A bearing is an angle measured from a **north line** in a **clockwise direction**. We sometimes call bearings '**three figure bearings**' because there must always be three figures. If the angle measures

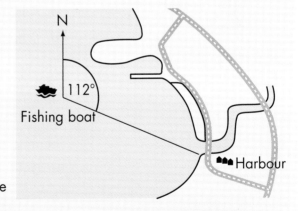

less than 100° then the value is still written using three figures. For example, with an angle of 43° the bearing is 043°.

In the diagram, the bearing of the harbour from the fishing boat is 112°.

Example 5.1

What is the bearing of the tower from the car park?

The important word in the question is 'from'. This tells us where to measure our angle. We first need to have a north line to measure from.

Draw a north line at the car park. To do this, draw a line parallel to the north line on the map, going through the • indicating the position of the car park.

Join the tower and the car park with a straight line. Extend the line so that you can use a protractor.

Use a protractor to measure the angle from the north line to the straight line that you have drawn.

This measures 53° so the bearing is 053°.

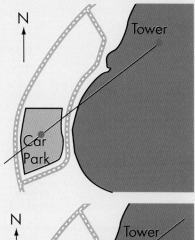

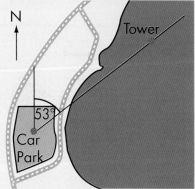

Exercise 5d

SUS5d

1 A, B, C and D are four ships at different positions at sea. Draw appropriate north lines on SUS5d and use a protractor to find the bearing of:

a A from B **b** B from C **c** D from B

d D from C **e** C from D.

2 The map of part of the coastline on SUS5d shows the position of a ship S and a harbour H. The scale of the map is 1 : 40 000.

The ship sails on a bearing of 220° for 2.5 km and then on a bearing of 330° for 3.2 km.

a Draw the ship's course on the diagram.

b How far is the ship from the harbour now and what bearing does it have to sail on to get there?

3 Three ships at sea (the *Nina*, the *Pinta* and the *Santa Maria*) form an equilateral triangle with sides of 19 km. The *Nina* is south west of the *Pinta*.

  a Draw a scale diagram showing the positions of the three ships. Use a scale of 2 cm = 1 km.

  b Use your diagram to find the bearing of the *Santa Maria* from the Pinta.

  c Use your diagram to find the bearing of the *Santa Maria* from the *Nina*.

  The *Pinta* and the *Nina* are anchored, i.e. not moving. The *Santa Maria* sails on a bearing of 035°.

  d How far does it need to sail so that it is due east of the *Pinta*?

  e How far due east of the *Pinta* is it at that moment?

Activity Sheet 5.3

Activity 5.3

Consolidation Exercise

SUSCE1

1 The recipe to make a fruit smoothie to serve six people is shown.

4 ripe peaches 8 tbsp Greek yoghurt
60 g of frozen blueberries 6 brazil nuts
60 g of frozen strawberries
2 medium bananas

Write this recipe to serve:

  a 12 people   **b** 9 people   **c** 15 people.

2 Copy and complete the table showing ratios used for some enlargements.

	Ratio	Old measurement	New measurement
a	1 : 8	2 cm	
b	3 : 5	30 mm	
c		16 cm	40 cm
d	4 : 5		35 cm
e	10 : 3		3 cm
f		24 cm	15 cm

3 Rory uses a map of the Londonderry area with a scale of 1 : 50 000. He measures these straight line distances on the map.

Greysteel Railway Bridge to Carrickhugh Railway Bridge 7.8 cm

Summit of Eglish to summit of Slievekirk 13.3 cm

Bonds Glen Gravel Pit to Standing Stones at Kilcaltan 6.4 cm

Find the actual straight line distances between these places.

4 The table shows some map scales written in two different ways. Copy and complete the table.

a	b	c	d	e
1 : 100	1 : 1000	1 : 500		1 : 20 000
1 cm = _ m	1 cm = __ m	1 cm = __ m	1 cm = 500 m	1 cm = __ km

5 The map on SUSCE1 shows some features in a mountain area.

A group of walkers sets off from the sheepfold, walks to Drinns summit, then to Williams Hill and back to the sheepfold.

Copy and complete the table detailing their journey.

Leg of journey	Bearing	Actual distance
a Sheepfold to Drinns Summit		
b Drinns Summit to Williams Hill		
c Williams Hill to sheepfold		

6 a An image is enlarged so that its new length is $4\frac{1}{2}$ times its old length.

What is the ratio of this enlargement, in its simplest form?

b An image is 16 cm long and is reduced so that its new length is 10 cm.

What is the ratio of this reduction?

7 A ship travels on a bearing of 285° for 3.5 km. It changes direction to 045° and travels for 6.7 km.

a Draw an accurate diagram to show the ship's course. Use a scale of 1 : 50 000. Start by placing an × in the centre of a blank sheet of paper to represent the ship.

b Use your diagram to find how far the ship is from its original position.

c On what bearing would the ship need to sail to return to its original position?

Handling data

Discussion 6.1

Ryan is investigating the weights (masses) of pebbles on the beach as part of his environmental science project. He records the distance from the shoreline for 12 pebbles and then finds the mass of each one.

Ryan draws this **scatter graph**.

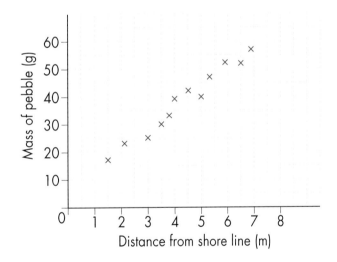

What is the mass of the heaviest pebble?

One pebble was 4 m from the shoreline. What was the mass of that pebble?

What can you say about the weight of pebbles as you move away from the shoreline?

This scatter graph shows **positive correlation** – as one variable increases, so does the other. Name some more variables that might have positive correlation.

A **scatter graph** shows the relationship between two variables.

We can use a scatter graph to help us comment on the **correlation** between the **variables**.

The diagrams show possible types of correlation.

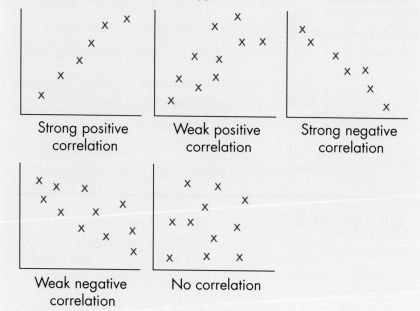

Strong positive correlation

Weak positive correlation

Strong negative correlation

Weak negative correlation

No correlation

Exercise 6a

1 For each scatter graph shown, describe the correlation between the variables.

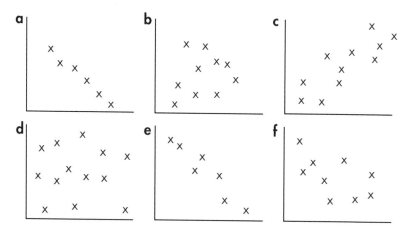

a

b

c

d

e

f

2 The table shows the number of units of electricity used in 15 households and the number of people living in each house.

Number in household	5	4	4	2	3	5	6	4	3	2	4	5	8	3	1
Units used per day	15	12	11	8	9	10	14	12	8	8	10	14	18	10	7

a Draw a scatter graph to show this information.

b Comment on the correlation.

3 Oliver thinks that a 500 ml bottle of water is more expensive the closer you get to the football stadium in his town. He visits 15 shops within 4 km of the stadium and notes the price of a 500 ml bottle of water and the distance from the stadium.

Distance from stadium (km)	3.2	0.8	1	1.5	0	1.7	2.8	3.7	0.6	3.4	1.1	0.2	1.9	2.3	3.5
Price of water (pence)	79	65	45	75	105	62	72	55	65	79	85	100	70	59	69

a Draw a scatter graph to show this information.

b Was Oliver correct? Use the correlation in your scatter graph to justify your answer.

4 As part of a class survey, Tina asks 12 people who have a computer in her class to record how long they spent doing homework and how long they used the computer for fun on a particular school night.

Time spent on homework (minutes)	82	42	47	44	45	72	40	35	42	65	45	25
Time on computer (minutes)	21	148	80	63	45	51	120	90	100	30	150	170

a Draw a scatter graph to show this information.

b Tina thinks that there is no connection between how long pupils spend on the computer and how long they spend on homework. Is she correct?

Use the correlation in your scatter graph to justify your answer.

5 As part of her GCSE geography river study, Joanne measures the speed of a river and its width in 10 places along its length.

Width of river (m)	0.7	1.2	1.5	1.9	2.2	2.3	2.7	2.9	3.1	3.3
Speed of river (m/s)	2.9	2.5	2.2	1.7	1.6	1.4	1.4	1.1	0.9	0.7

a Draw a scatter graph to show this information.

b Comment on the correlation.

c Write a sentence to link the width of the river and its speed.

6 The table shows the length and width of some leaves from the same tree.

Length of leaf (cm)	6.7	3.2	4.7	5.4	5.0	4.9	3.8	4.1	3.4	5.8	6.3	4.6	6.3	6.0	5.2
Width of leaf (cm)	3.8	1.3	2.6	3.2	2.9	2.6	2.2	2.5	1.8	3.5	3.2	2.5	3.7	3.4	3.3

a Draw a scatter graph to show this information.

b Comment on the correlation.

c Write a sentence to link the length and width of the leaves.

Discussion 6.2

Ryan wants to do some further work on his scatter graph. He draws a **line of best fit**.

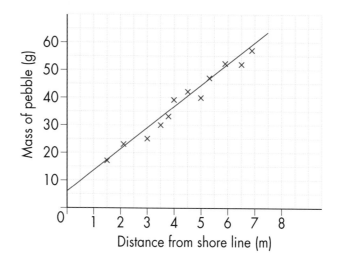

Describe how the line of best fit has been drawn.

Ryan has another pebble that weighs 25 g but he has forgotten to measure the distance from the shoreline. How could he use the line of best fit to estimate the distance from the shoreline?

Another pebble was collected 10.5 m from the shoreline. Use the line of best fit to estimate the weight (mass) of the pebble.

A line of best fit is a straight line that best fits the data.

The line of best fit should:

- have approximately the same number of data points on either side

- follow the trend of the data.

The line of best fit may go through one, several or none of the data points.

To help you draw a line of best fit, use a ruler on its edge to divide the points.

Exercise 6b

You will need your scatter graphs from Exercise 6a for this Exercise.

1   Which of these lines are not lines of best fit? For each line explain why you think it is a line of best fit or not.

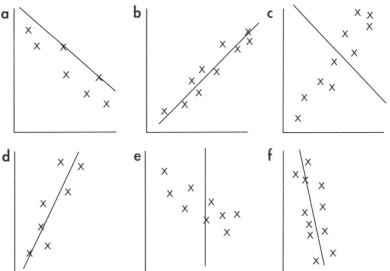

2   For this question, use your scatter graph from question **2** in Exercise 6a.

   a   Draw a line of best fit on your scatter graph.

   b   Another household has seven people. Use your line of best fit to find approximately how many units of electricity you would expect them to use per day.

3   For this question, use your scatter graph from question **4** in Exercise 6a.

   a   Draw a line of best fit on your scatter graph.

   b   Another pupil spent 1 hour on her computer but forgot to record how long she spent doing homework. Use your line of best fit to estimate how long she spent on her homework.

   c   Using evidence from your line of best fit, how long would you expect a pupil to spend on homework if he does not use his computer at all?

4   For this question, use your scatter graph from question **5** in Exercise 6a.

   a   Draw a line of best fit on your scatter graph.

   b   At a certain point Joanne measures the speed of the river as 2 m/s but cannot get to the other side to measure the width. Use your line of best fit to estimate the width at that point.

   c   What would you expect the speed of the river to be when the width is 1 m?

   d   Could you use your line of best fit to estimate the speed of the river when the width is 4.5 metres?

5 For this question, use your scatter graph from question **6** in Exercise 6a.

a Draw a line of best fit on your scatter graph.

b Use your line of best fit to copy and complete the table.

Estimated length of leaf (cm)	6.5		
Estimated width of leaf (cm)		2.4	3.6

Activity
Sheet 6.1

Activity 6.1

Discussion 6.3

Protein	4%
Carbohydrates	80%
Fat	10%
Fibre	3%
Other	3%

The table gives nutritional information about a cereal bar.

Cameron and Lewis are working together to draw a pie chart from this table.

They need to know the sizes of the angles to draw for each section of the pie chart.

Cameron thinks that you need to draw angles of 4°, 80°, 10°, 3° and 3°.

Can you explain why this is not correct?

Lewis also thinks that Cameron is wrong. He says 'It is easy to work out the angle for 10% because 10% is the same as one tenth. You need $\frac{1}{10}$ of a circle to represent 10%.

360 ÷ 10 = 36. You need an angle of 36° for the fat section of the pie chart.'

Work with a partner and use Lewis's method to work out the rest of the angles for the pie chart.

Exercise 6c

1 Draw the pie chart using the data from Discussion 6.3. Label each section – you do not need to write the sizes of the angles on your pie chart. Remember to give your pie chart a title.

2 The table shows the percentages of different ingredients in a Deep Pan Veggie Pizza.

Crust	Cheese	Tomato sauce	Peppers	Mushrooms
60%	20%	10%	5%	5%

Draw and label a pie chart to show this information.

3 The owner of a small factory has worked out that the cost of manufacturing soft toys is made up as follows.

Overheads	45%
Raw materials	35%
Wages	15%
Other costs	5%

Draw and label a pie chart to show this information.

4 A council records the weight of different materials collected for recycling. The table shows the percentages of each type of material collected.

Compost	Glass	Textiles	Other materials	Plastic	Cans	Metals	Paper
36%	10%	4%	22.5%	2%	3.5%	12.5%	9.5%

Draw and label a pie chart to show this information.

5 The percentages of the population that live in each of the six counties of Northern Ireland are: Antrim 29%, Down 26%, Londonderry 16%, Armagh 16%, Tyrone 8% and Fermanagh 5%.

Draw and label a pie chart to show this information. Round the angles to the nearest whole number, where necessary.

6 The data for pie charts is not always given in percentages. Sometimes the actual amounts are given. First copy the table and complete the working out for each angle, and then draw the pie chart for household expenditure.

Household bill	Amount spent	Angle
Mortgage	£53	53 ÷ 200 × 360° = 95.4° Round to 95°
Transport	£60	
Food	£45	
Clothes/footwear	£24	
Fuel	£18	
Total	£200	

Discussion 6.4

Cameron and Lewis are answering questions about a pie chart showing nutritional information for another cereal bar.

The first question asks what percentage of the cereal bar is carbohydrate.

Cameron now knows that an angle of 252° does not mean that 252% of the cereal bar is carbohydrate!

He says, 'The fraction of the pie chart for carbohydrate is $\frac{252}{360}$ so we need to multiply $\frac{252}{360}$ by 100 to find the percentage'.

$252 \div 360 \times 100\% = 70\%$

Is Cameron correct?

Work with a partner to calculate the percentages for the rest of the pie chart.

Cereal bar information

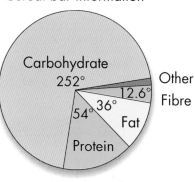

Exercise 6d

1 The pie chart shows the types of music CDs borrowed from a library during a particular month.

   a What fraction of the CDs were Pop CDs?

   b What percentage of the CDs were Pop CDs?

   c Calculate the percentages for the other types of music CDs.

Types of music

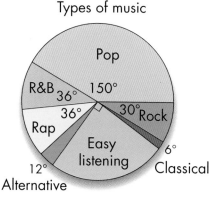

2 At a large office, 180 people were asked how many minutes it had taken them to travel to work that day. The results are shown in the pie chart.

Copy and complete the table.

Number of minutes taken

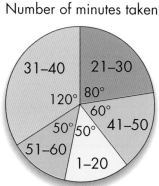

Time taken (minutes)	1–20	21–30	31–40	41–50	51–60
Number of people					

3 The pie chart shows what a plate should look like for a balanced meal.

Calculate the percentages of each of the food types.

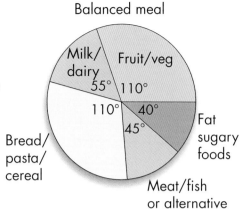

Balanced meal

Milk/dairy 55°
Fruit/veg 110°
110°
40°
45°
Fat sugary foods
Bread/pasta/cereal
Meat/fish or alternative

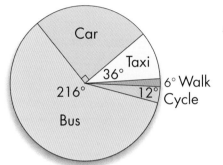

Car
Taxi 36°
6° Walk
216°
12° Cycle
Bus

4 The pie chart shows the results of a survey on how people in a shopping centre travelled there on a particular day.

Six people travelled by taxi.

a How many people got the bus to the shopping centre?

b How many people were surveyed altogether?

Activity
Sheet 6.2

Activity 6.2

Discussion 6.5

The times taken for 17 students to complete an ICT task (in minutes) are shown.

25 28 19 17 8 9 30 15 12 9 10

22 10 21 11 33 22

The data can be represented by a stem and leaf diagram.

```
0 | 8  9  9
1 | 0  0  1  2  5  7  9
2 | 1  2  2  5  8
3 | 0  3
```

Key: 2|5 means 25

The stems are 0, 1, 2 and 3. What numbers are the leaves?

What was the shortest time taken to complete the task?

What was the longest time taken to complete the task?

What was the modal time taken to complete the ICT task?

What was the median time taken to complete the ICT task?

What are the advantages of arranging the data as a stem and leaf diagram?

Exercise 6e

1   A traffic survey measures the speeds of vehicles going past a certain point on a dual carriageway. The speeds (in miles per hour (mph)) recorded for vehicles between 2 p.m. and 2.05 p.m. are shown on a stem and leaf diagram.

```
4 | 2   6   7
5 | 0   5   6   6   7   8   8   9   9
6 | 1   3   3   5   6   6
7 | 2
```

Key 5 | 6 means 56 mph

a   How many cars went past the point between 2 p.m. and 2.05 p.m.?

b   The speed limit on this dual carriageways is 60 mph. How many of these vehicles were breaking the speed limit?

c   What was the median speed recorded?

2   The speeds of vehicles (in miles per hour) going past the same point (from question 1) between 5 p.m. and 5.05 p.m. are shown.

56 61 54 43 57 44 58 48 56 61 59 48

52 63 47 57 59 61 50 55 60 54 59 58

a   Draw a stem and leaf diagram of this data. Don't forget to include a key.

b   What was the median speed recorded?

c   One reason for doing the survey was to find out if drivers drive faster during the rush hour than at other times of the day. What is your opinion, based on the evidence from your stem and leaf diagram and the one from question 1?

3   The amounts raised by some children taking part in a sponsored Mathsathon are shown in the stem and leaf diagram.

```
3 | 25   37   50   50
4 | 20   38   50   50   75   80   93
5 | 00   00   20   25   25   50   50   75   82   90
6 | 00   00   50
```

Key 5 | 25 means £5.25

a   How many children raised more than £5?

b   What was the median amount raised?

4 The times taken for 17 runners from a local team to complete the Belfast Marathon are shown.

Name	Time	Name	Time
Julie	3h 14 minutes	Martin	3h 26 minutes
Joseph	4h 11 minutes	Maria	4h 25 minutes
Gerry	5h 7 minutes	Barry	3h 31 minutes
Jane	2h 55 minutes	Peter	3h 52 minutes
Ryan	3h 12 minutes	Pat	2h 38 minutes
Ruth	4h 3 minutes	Kathryn	3h 35 minutes
James	5h 7 minutes	Kate	4h 47 minutes
Scott	2h 42 minutes	Steven	3h 40 minutes
Audrey	3h 38 minutes		

    a Draw a stem and leaf diagram to show the runners' times.

    b One of the runners says that he did better than 75% of these runners. Which runner could this have been?

5 The **back-to-back stem and leaf diagram** shows the ages of people attending a tai chi class and the ages of people attending an aerobics evening class.

Tai chi   **Aerobics**

```
                        1 | 8  8
                9   2 | 2  3  6  7   7   8
              9   7   3 | 0  3  5  7
        8  4  4  2   4 | 2  5  6
  8  7  7  5  1   5 | 0  2
        7  4  2   6 | 3
              3   7 | 1
```

Key 7 | 3 means 37   4 | 2 means 42

    a How many people in their 40s attend the aerobics class?

    b What was the median age for the tai chi?

    c What was the median age for the aerobics class?

    d Write a few sentences to compare the ages of the people attending these classes.

Activity
Sheet 6.3

Activity 6.3

Consolidation Exercise

Age (years)	Time (minutes)	Age (years)	Time (minutes)
18	3	29	5.5
24	4.5	33	6
21	3.5	40	7.5
52	6.5	59	10.5
35	4	63	9
46	8	24	4
40	7	72	11
42	8	48	12
35	6.5	55	8.5
27	5	61	9

Cinema visit	25%
Magazines	7.5%
Savings	
Cosmetics	15%
Clothes	40%

80.3	76.6	75.5	70.1
81.0	67.6	69.4	72.0
72.3	68.5	74.4	77.9
82.4	64.2	73.9	62.7
81.5	79.4	77.7	65.2

1 For each of these pairs of variables, state whether you would expect to find positive, negative or no correlation.

   a Time a person takes to run 100 m and time they take to run 200 m.

   b Temperature and number of people on the beach.

   c Score in non-calculator maths test and score in mental maths test.

   d Number of miles driven and number of litres of petrol used.

   e Time spent in shower and number of litres of water used.

   f Height of person and amount spent on holiday.

2 In a study, 20 people who regularly use e-mail were asked to compose and send a given 20-word e-mail with an attachment on the same computer. The time taken (to the nearest 0.5 minutes) and the ages of the people are shown.

   a Draw a scatter graph to show this information and describe the correlation.

   b Draw a line of best fit on your scatter graph and use it to estimate the time that a 30-year-old person who regularly uses e-mail would take.

   c Estimate the age of a person who takes 10 minutes to send the e-mail.

3 The table shows how Stephanie spent her pocket money one week.

   a What percentage of her pocket money did Stephanie save?

   b Draw a pie chart to show this information.

   c Stephanie's friend Jody also drew a pie chart to show how she had spent her pocket money that week. The angle for 'clothes' was the same on both pie charts. Stephanie says that she and Jody must have spent the same amount on clothes that week. Explain why Stephanie may not be correct.

4 The weights (in kg) of the first team squad of a football team are shown on the left.

   Draw a stem and leaf diagram to show the footballers' weights and find the median weight of these footballers.

5 The number of texts sent on a particular day by 20 teenage boys and the number sent by 20 teenage girls are shown.

Number of texts (Boys)	11	4	6	8	12	23	18	19	5	7	3	2	14	20	9	12	8	4	17	10
Number of texts (Girls)	15	23	32	14	25	17	10	21	16	9	5	12	24	28	21	17	19	30	24	22

Draw a back-to-back stem and leaf diagram of this information and write a short paragraph about what the stem and leaf diagram tells you.

Task 1: Population data

Here are some facts and figures about the population of the United Kingdom.

- In mid-2007 the resident population of the UK was 60 975 000.

- The mean age was 39 years.

- Children aged under 16 represented around 20% of the total population.

- The proportion of retirement age was also around 20% of the total population.

- Up to the age of 72, the number of males and females are fairly equal.

- From the age of 73 onwards, females outnumber males of the same age.

The extract from a spreadsheet on SUSTask1 shows ages of the population of Northern Ireland for June 2006.

Use this information to compare the age structure of the population of Northern Ireland with that of the whole of the UK.

You will need to compare each of the statements above and write about your findings.

You could also find some more information points about the population of the UK and use them to compare with Northern Ireland.

You should start with a plan of your work, giving reasons for any mathematical methods that you choose. It is also important to work accurately and to show all your working out.

7 Decimals

- understand significant figures
- calculate and estimate involving multiplication and division of numbers up to three decimal places
- calculate and estimate square roots to an appropriate degree of accuracy
- understand and use the method of trial and improvement.

Discussion 7.1

The population of Northern Ireland in June 2006 was estimated to be 1 741 649 people. Jacob rounds this number to 1 700 000 and says that this is the population accurate to two **significant figures**. What do you think this means? What is the population to one significant figure? Jenny thinks the population rounded to four significant figures is 1742. What mistake has she made?

The average price for a litre of diesel, in September 2008, across Northern Ireland was 121.04p. To how many significant figures has this price been given? What is this amount to one significant figure? Would this be a sensible estimate to use? What estimate would be appropriate to use for the price of a litre of diesel?

Small numbers are slightly different. **Leading zeros** are not significant. What is the first significant figure of 0.0024? Round 0.0024 to one significant figure. What is 0.095 to one significant figure?

Jamie is confused. He has been asked to round 1000.0004 to four significant figures. Jamie says it isn't possible as there are only two significant figures. Can you help him?

Example 7.1

Round **a** 123 678 to three significant figures

b 0.005344 to two significant figures

a <u>123</u> 678   124 <u>000</u>

these are   the 4th significant   these zeros are added
the first 3   figure is at least 5   to maintain the size of
significant   so the 3 must be   the number
figures   rounded up to 4

b 0.00<u>5</u> 344   0.00<u>5</u> 3

these are   the 3rd significant   these zeros must be
the first two   figure is less than 5 so   kept to maintain the
significant   the 2nd figure remains   size of the number
figures   unchanged at 3

Exercise 7a

1 Bob weighs 91.75 kg. Which figure is the most significant and what is its value?

2 Round the following numbers to one significant figure (1 s.f.).

    a 22   **b** 550   **c** 999

    d 76 395   **e** 0.247   **f** 0.055

3 Round these numbers to two significant figures.

    a 543 641   **b** 2.8462   **c** 16 501

    d 0.7962   **e** 28.71   **f** 0.0544

4 Round these numbers to three significant figures.

    a 7420   **b** 86.94   **c** 0.008248

    d 614.09   **e** 0.8005   **f** 2 877 462

5 Round 0.007958257 to **a** one significant figure **b** two significant figures **c** three significant figures **d** four significant figures.

6 The diameter of a human hair was measured as 0.00254 cm. Round this to one significant figure.

7 **a** Round 704 795 to four significant figures.

    b Round 704 795 to five significant figures.

    c What do you notice about the answers to **a** and **b**? Explain why this is the case.

8 The number of students in a school rounded to two significant figures (2 s.f.) is 1300. What is the least and greatest possible number of students in this school?

9 The label on a jar containing 50 sweets states that the contents are correct to one significant figure. What is the least and greatest number of sweets in the jar?

Activity 7.1

Discussion 7.2

Why is it important to be able to estimate when doing a weekly shop in a supermarket? To what amount would it be sensible to round the cost of a pack of sausages at £1.59? A can of baked beans costing 43p? A pack of washing powder costing £7.79? Why might some people prefer to estimate this price to one significant figure rather than to two significant figures? How would you estimate the total cost of seven cans of cat food costing 57p each?

Why do some people prefer to shop in the more expensive whole food markets or farmers' markets?

Exercise 7b

1 Sara visited two supermarkets and a farmer's shop to compare prices for 10 items on her shopping list. The prices and items are shown in the table.

	Tasco	Asta	MacDonald's farm shop
Ham, cheese and pickle sandwich	£1.59	£1.37	£2.45
Tuna salad	£2.07	£1.83	£3.12
1 litre orange juice	£0.78	£0.65	£1.09
Fruit salad tub	£1.61	£1.78	£2.37
Plain crisps	£0.32	£0.27	£0.46
Yoghurt	£0.82	£0.75	£1.49
Wholemeal bread	£1.21	£1.02	£1.54
Golden delicious apples (6 pack)	£1.32	£1.27	£1.88
Rhubarb	£1.97	£1.72	£2.25
Milk (2 litres)	£1.39	£1.20	£1.66

Find the total cost of the items in

a Tasco   b Asta   c MacDonald's farm shop.

d Round each of the prices to one significant figure and find the estimated totals for each of the stores.

e Comment on the suitability of these estimates.

f Round each of the prices to two significant figures and find the estimated totals for each of the stores.

g Comment on the suitability of these estimates.

h Describe a more useful method of estimation for prices such as those given.

2 The speed of light is 299 792 458 metres per second. Round this to an appropriate degree of accuracy.

3 The heights of the highest mountains in Northern Ireland are shown.

Rank	Mountain	Height (m)
1	Slieve Donard	849
2	Slieve Commedagh	767
3	Slieve Binnian	747
4	Slieve Bearnagh	727
5=	Slieve Lamagan	704
5=	Slieve Mael Beg	704
7	Slieve Mael Mor	682
8	Sawel Mountain	678
9	Slieve Muck	674
10	Shan Slieve	671

a If each mountain's height was rounded to two significant figures how many different heights would there be?

b Which mountains have the same height when rounded to two significant figures?

4 The estimated population of the counties in Northern Ireland is shown below.

County Antrim: 616 048   County Armagh: 147 990
County Down: 479 037   County Fermanagh: 59 222
County Londonderry: 212 862   County Tyrone: 186 516

Round each county's population to three significant figures.

5 The approximate wavelengths of the colours in the rainbow are given below.

Red 0.000 665 mm   Orange 0.000 617 mm
Yellow 0.000 572 mm   Green 0.000 522 mm
Blue 0.000 473 mm   Indigo 0.000 445 mm
Violet 0.000 421 mm

a To how many significant figures have each of these wavelengths been given?

b Explain why it would be inappropriate to round each wavelength to one significant figure.

c Round each wavelength to two significant figures. Would this be an appropriate degree of accuracy?

Activity Sheet 7.2

Activity 7.2

Sometimes, when dividing numbers, the answer is not exact and it will be necessary to round to a suitable number of decimal places.

Example 7.2

a Find 31 divided by 7 correct to three decimal places using a calculator.

b Find $37 \div 7$ correct to three decimal places without using a calculator.

a $31 \div 7 = 4.428571429$, which rounds to 4.429 to 3 d.p.

b We want three decimal places, so find the digits in the first four decimal places.

$$
\begin{array}{r}
5.2857 \\
7\overline{)37.0000}^{2\,6\,4\,5}
\end{array}
$$

Since the figure in the 4th decimal place, 7, is 5 or more, the digit in the 3rd decimal place must be rounded up from 5 to 6.

So $37 \div 7$ correct to three decimal places is 5.286.

Exercise 7c

1 Find the answers to these questions correct to the given number of decimal places (d.p.). Do not use a calculator.

    a $2.7 \div 6$ (1 d.p.)   **b** $22.07 \div 5$ (2 d.p.)

    c $0.19 \div 3$ (3 d.p.)   **d** $20.1 \div 8$ (3 d.p.)

    e $19 \div 7$ (2 d.p.)   **f** $223 \div 11$ (3 d.p.)

2 Calculate the answers to these questions. Write down the full calculator display for each answer first and then round each answer correct to the given number of decimal places.

    a $0.87 \div 4.05$ (3 d.p.)   **b** $362 \div 777$ (2 d.p.)

    c $25.008 \div 24.72$ (1 d.p.)

3 Jamie calculates the area of a rectangle as 54.275 m². If the length of the rectangle is 6.75 m, what is the breadth?

4 What is $\frac{1}{8}$ of $\frac{1}{4}$ to **a** one decimal place **b** one significant figure? Which value is more useful?

Activity 7.3

Activity Sheet 7.3

Discussion 7.3

Conor says 17.5 times 42.6 is 7455. Anna-Marie thinks it should be 745.5. How could you quickly check which answer is sensible?

It is always a good idea to **estimate** answers to problems even if a calculator is being used, so that mistakes can be identified.

Joyce divides £24 157 by 812 to find the average ticket price for a concert. She gets an answer of £297.50 which seems very expensive for a ticket. What could she have done wrong? Use estimation to help Joyce find a more realistic average ticket price.

Ross bought 22 000 screws costing £2.37 per thousand. Estimate how much he spent in total.

Exercise 7d

1 A house for sale is advertised as having a master bedroom of size 4.23 m by 3.18 m.

  a Estimate the area of the bedroom.

  b Is your estimate an overestimate or an underestimate? Explain your answer.

  c Use a calculator to find the area of the room. Give your answer to an appropriate degree of accuracy.

2 Estimate answers to each of these by rounding all values to one significant figure. Show your method clearly. The first one has been done for you.

  a 28.72 × 205.46: Estimate 30 × 200 = 6000

  b 521 × 78   **c** 72 205 × 23.2

  d 2.855 × 0.48   **e** 8122 × 15.84

  f 84500 ÷ 81.9   **g** 54.02 ÷ 0.955

  h 612.3 ÷ 2.79   **i** 74 658.1 ÷ 187.52

  j 0.042 ÷ 4.08

3 **a i** Estimate the answer to 3477 × 24.2 by rounding each of the numbers to one significant figure.

   ii What is the exact answer? Comment.

  b i Estimate the answer to 152.7 × 56.2 by rounding each of the numbers to one significant figure.

   ii What is the exact answer? Comment.

  c i Estimate the answer to 74.87 ÷ 14.62 by rounding each of the numbers to one significant figure.

   ii What is the exact answer? Comment.

  d Write down a division which gives an underestimate when each of the numbers is rounded to one significant figure.

4 Use estimates to find which of the answers are likely to be wrong.

  a $478 \times 9 = 5302$ **b** $77.5 \times 6.4 = 496$

  c $2055 \div 3 = 685$ **d** $394.8 \div 7 = 66.4$

5 Estimate the answers to the following by rounding all figures to one significant figure.

  a $310 + 47 + 8.6$ **b** $72\,566 + 145\,809$

  c Which of the estimates is poor? Give reasons.

  d How could you improve this estimate?

Activity 7.4

Activity Sheet 7.4

Activity 7.5

Activity Sheet 7.5

Discussion 7.4

Mr Hamilton fills his car with petrol costing 105.9p per litre. He buys 38.64 litres. Estimate the total cost of the petrol. Use a calculator to find the cost to the nearest penny.

Estimate the answer to $\frac{38 + 79}{3.7}$. Use your calculator to find the answer correct to two decimal places. Marie got the wrong answer to this problem but can't understand why. She entered the following into her calculator.

What has she done wrong? How would you advise Marie to perform this calculation?

Why is it always sensible to estimate the answer before using a calculator?

Use your calculator to find the value of the following. Round your answers to two decimal places, where appropriate.
11.04^2 0.377^3 $\sqrt{30}$ $\sqrt[3]{58.25}$

Use the bracket keys on your calculator to help you work out the value of $(5.37 + 2.08) \times 2.77$.

Exercise 7e

1 Use the bracket keys on your calculator to work out the following. Write down what you input each time.

   a $\dfrac{8.2 + 7.3}{24.2 - 16.8}$ b $\dfrac{28.87 - 6.2^2}{-25 \times 0.78}$ c $5.28 - \dfrac{4.6}{2.07 + 2.85}$

2 For each of these questions

   a estimate the answer

   b write down how you would input the calculation into your calculator

   c use your calculator to find the answer correct to two decimal places.

   i $(33 \times 47) - (57 \times 12)$ ii $\dfrac{12.37 + 9.13}{2.7}$

   iii $\dfrac{23.6 \times 7.44}{12.4 - (2.8 - 0.96)}$ iv $\dfrac{-6.4 \times 27.5}{1.87 + 13.34}$

3 a Estimate an answer to $\dfrac{3.12\,(12^2 - 136)}{21.5 + 44.8}$ by rounding all values to one significant figure. Is this a sensible estimate?

   b Try to find a better estimate and write down your method.

   c Use your calculator to find the answer correct to two decimal places.

4 Calculate the values of the following correct to two decimal places.

   a $(22.5 - 19.08)^3 - \sqrt{47.2}$ b $\sqrt{\dfrac{14.8 \times 2.33}{0.05}} - 3.08^3$

   c $\sqrt[3]{(21.7 - 3.7)^2}$

5 Find the square root of each of the fractions correct to three decimal places.

   a $\frac{11}{17}$ b $\frac{34}{53}$ c $\frac{7}{11}$ d $\frac{247}{384}$

Example 7.3

Use the method of **trial and improvement** to estimate the square root of 150 accurate to 1 decimal place.

Step 1 Find the two whole numbers between which $\sqrt{150}$ lies.

$12^2 = 144$, $13^2 = 169$: $\sqrt{150}$ is between 12 and 13.

Step 2 Find two values, to one decimal place, between which the solution lies.

As 150 is closer to 144 than 169, try a value closer to 12 than 13.

Try 12.3.

$12.3^2 = 151.29$ This is too high, so choose a smaller value.

Try 12.2

$12.2^2 = 148.84$ This is too low, so $\sqrt{150}$ lies between 12.2 and 12.3.

Step 3 Test the mid-point of 12.2 and 12.3.

$12.25^2 = 150.0625$: This is too high.

Step 4 Round up or down.

Since 12.25^2 is too high round down to 12.2.

$\sqrt{150}$ is 12.2 accurate to one decimal place.

Exercise 7f

1 Matthew is finding the square root of 41. His method is shown.

$$6^2 = 36 \text{ too low}$$
$$7^2 = 49 \text{ too high}$$
$$6.3^2 = 39.69 \text{ too low}$$
$$6.4^2 = 40.96 \text{ too low}$$
$$6.5^2 = 42.25 \text{ too high}$$
$$6.45^2 = 41.6025 \text{ too high}$$

What is $\sqrt{41}$ accurate to one decimal place?

2 Michael is finding the square root of 350. This is the start of his working.

Complete the solution for Michael and write down your answer accurate to one decimal place.

$$18^2 = 324 \text{ too low}$$
$$19^2 = 361 \text{ too high}$$
$$18.7^2 = 349.69 \text{ too low}$$
$$18.8^2 = 353.44 \text{ too high}$$

3 David is finding the square root of 258 but has become confused. His method is shown.

a Why is David confused? What value should he test next?

b Complete the solution for David and write down your answer correct to one decimal place.

$$16^2 = 256 \text{ too low}$$
$$17^2 = 289 \text{ too high}$$
$$16.1^2 = 259.21 \text{ too high}$$

4 Use the method of trial and improvement to estimate the following square roots accurate to one decimal place. Show all of your method.

a $\sqrt{12}$ **b** $\sqrt{80}$ **c** $\sqrt{110}$

d $\sqrt{200}$ **e** $\sqrt{214.7}$ **f** $\sqrt{1.27}$

5 The area of a square is $566\,cm^2$. Use the method of trial and improvement to find the length of a side to the nearest mm.

Activity
Sheet 7.6

Activity 7.6

Discussion 7.5

The area of a square garage floor is 16.95 m². How could you find the length of each side of the garage floor using a calculator? Jamie uses his calculator and says the length of each side is 4.117 037 77 m. What is the problem with this answer? What would a more appropriate answer be?

Exercise 7g

Calculate the following square roots to the given degree of accuracy.

1 $\sqrt{476}$ (3 s.f.)
2 $\sqrt{529}$ (1 s.f.)
3 $\sqrt{5.87}$ (2 s.f.)
4 $\sqrt{1248}$ (5 s.f.)
5 $\sqrt{222875}$ (2 d.p.)

6 $\sqrt{1.058}$ (2 s.f.)
7 $\sqrt{0.8}$ (1 d.p.)
8 $\sqrt{0.775}$ (3 s.f.)
9 $\sqrt{20.54}$ (4 s.f.)
10 $\sqrt{0.1}$ (1 s.f.)

Discussion 7.6

Trevor wants to make a brooch that has an area of 2000 mm². He wants to make a rectangular brooch that is 12 mm longer than it is wide. Help Trevor set up an equation to find the width and length of the brooch that he can make. Take the width of the brooch as x.

What will the length be in terms of x? The area of a rectangle is found by multiplying the length by the width.

width = x mm   length = $(x + 12)$ mm

The area of the brooch is 2000 mm².

area = width × length = 2000

      = $x (x + 12) = 2000$

Now expand the brackets.

area = $x^2 + 12x = 2000$

Example 7.4

To find x, the width of his brooch, accurate to one decimal place, Trevor uses the method of **trial and improvement**.

Value for x	x^2	$12x$	$x^2 + 12x$	
30	900	360	1260	too low
40	1600	480	2080	too high

So x lies between 30 and 40.

38	1444	456	1900	too low
39	1521	468	1989	too low

So x lies between 39 and 40.
(We already know the answer for $x = 40$)

39.1	1528.81	469.2	1998.01	too low
39.2	1536.64	470.4	2007.04	too high

So x lies between 39.1 and 39.2.

39.15	1532.7225	469.8	2002.5225	too high

So $x = 39.1$ to 1 decimal place.

The dimensions of Trevor's brooch are 39.1 mm wide and 51.1 mm long.

To check this answer is sensible find the area of the brooch. $39.1 \times 51.1 = 1998.01$. This is close to 2000 and therefore we can be confident about our answer.

Exercise 7h

1 Solve these equations for x, accurate to one decimal place. In each case a positive solution is required. The first one has been started for you.

  a $x^2 + 5x = 15$

   Try $x = 2$: $2^2 + (5 \times 2) = 4 + 10 = 14$ too low

   Try $x = 3$: $3^2 + (5 \times 3) = 9 + 15 = 24$ too high

   Try $x = 2.1$

  b $2x^2 - 3x = 16$ **c** $x(x + 10) = 61$

2 Solve $2x^2 + 5x = 20$ for x correct to one decimal place.

3 These problems have been started. Finish them off and find the value of x in each case accurate to one decimal place.

  a A rectangle is to be constructed with the following properties. The area is to be 40 cm². The length is to be three times the width. Let the width of the rectangle be x cm.

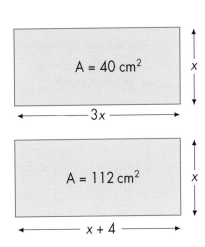

A = 40 cm²

3x

A = 112 cm²

x + 4

Sketch the rectangle and put on all information that is known.

Form an equation for the area of the rectangle in terms of x.

$3x \times x = 40$ giving $3x^2 = 40$.

Solve for x.

b Another rectangle is to be constructed with an area of 112 cm². The length is 4 cm longer than the width. The rectangle has been sketched with width x cm.

Form an equation in terms of x and solve.

**Activity
Sheet 7.7**

Activity 7.7

Consolidation Exercise

1 For 0.000 478 9 write down

  a the first significant figure   **b** the third significant figure.

2 Round these numbers to the given number of significant figures.

  a 62 877 (1 s.f.)   **b** 2 877 500 (1 s.f.)

  c 12 (1 s.f.)   **d** 0.002 78 (1 s.f.)

  e 27.49 (2 s.f.)   **f** 7.5068 (3 s.f.)

  g 50 049 (2 s.f.)   **h** 0.050 874 (3 s.f.)

  i 73.69 (2 s.f.)   **j** 2.999 95 (3 s.f.)

  k 1547 (2 s.f.)   **l** 27 897 452 (4 s.f.)

3 Manchester United played Barcelona over two legs in a knock out competition. The first leg had 70 048 spectators, while the second leg had 74 998 spectators.

  a What are the attendance figures to two significant figures?

  b What are these attendance figures to one significant figure? Is this a sensible degree of accuracy?

  c Julie is confused. She can't understand how the second leg attendance is 70 000 to one significant figure. She thinks 75 000 rounds to 80 000. What has Julie done wrong?

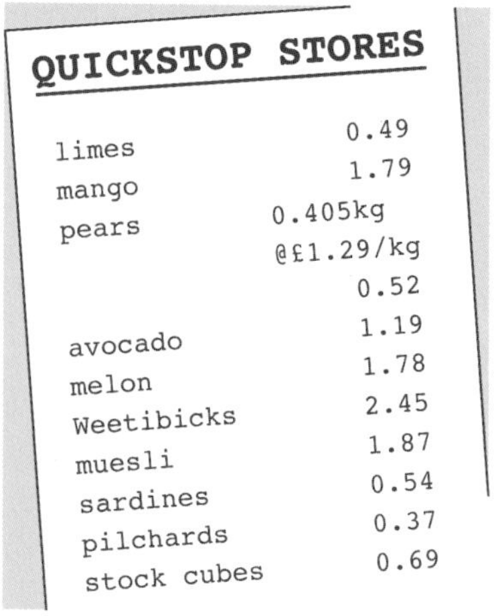

```
QUICKSTOP STORES

limes              0.49
mango              1.79
pears         0.405kg
              @£1.29/kg
                   0.52
                   1.19
avocado            1.78
melon              2.45
Weetibicks         1.87
muesli             0.54
sardines           0.37
pilchards          0.69
stock cubes
```

4 Estimate the volume of a cuboid with dimensions 32.8 cm by 17.8 cm by 11.4 cm by rounding each dimension to one significant figure.

5 Jack's stride is 77 cm long. If he walks 2.4 km, how many strides is this?

6 Estimate the cost of Emma's shopping bill (shown on the left). Round all amounts less than £1 to one significant figure and all amounts over £1 to two significant figures.

7 Use a calculator to work out the values of the following to the given degree of accuracy.

a 2.38×4.77 (3 s.f.)

b $8.254 \div 1.077$ (2 d.p.)

c 39.044×99.9 (4 s.f.)

d $3000 \div 1.8^2$ (3 d.p.)

e $0.328 \times 778 - 24.9$ (1 s.f.)

f $(2.449 - 3.97) \div 7.098$ (3 d.p.)

8 Solve the equations using the method of trial and improvement for positive values of x accurate to one decimal place.

a $x^2 + 3x = 8$

b $7x^2 - 3x = 47$

8 Shape

In this chapter, I am learning to:

- recognise and use rotational symmetry
- use co-ordinates in the four quadrants
- enlarge shapes about a given centre
- reflect shapes in a given line
- translate shapes.

Discussion 8.1

Look at the pictures. What is similar about these symbols?

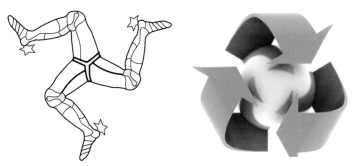

Do either of these shapes have lines of symmetry? Each of the symbols has rotational symmetry of order 3. What do you think this means? How could you check these orders of rotational symmetry?

The **centre of rotation** is the point that remains fixed throughout the rotation.

A shape is said to have **no rotational symmetry** if it only sits on top of itself once in a complete rotation.

Exercise 8a

SUS8a

1 Write down the order of rotational symmetry for each of the shapes below.

a   b   c   d 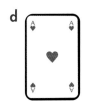   e   f   g   h

2 Trace the following shapes or logos from SUS8a and write down their order of rotational symmetry. Clearly mark the centre of rotation for each shape.

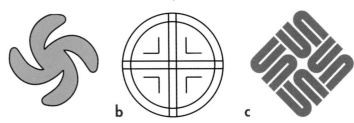

a   b   c

3 a What is the order of rotational symmetry of this shape?

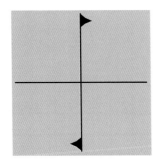

  b Redraw the shape so that it has rotational symmetry of order 4.

  c Use the shape to the right to draw diagrams that have orders of rotational symmetry of

i 2	**ii** 3	
iii 4	**iv** 6	

Take the point 'c' as the centre of each rotation.

4 a Copy or trace the arrangement below. Use SUS8a.

  b Is there any rotational symmetry? If so mark its centre and write the order.

  c Copy or trace the arrangement of letters below.

  d Is there rotational symmetry? If so mark its centre and write down the order.

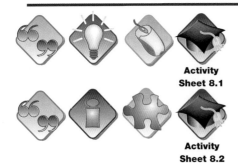

Activity Sheet 8.1

Activity 8.1

Activity Sheet 8.2

Activity 8.2

Discussion 8.2

Classify each of the triangles shown and state its order of rotational symmetry.

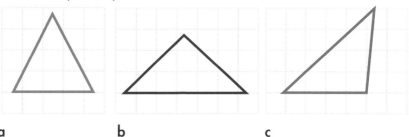

a   b   c

Kylie draws a triangle and says that its order of rotational symmetry isn't zero. Nick says that her triangle must have rotational symmetry of order 3. What do you think?

Which quadrilateral has rotational symmetry of order 4? Which quadrilaterals have rotational symmetry of order 2? Which quadrilaterals have no rotational symmetry? Can a quadrilateral have rotational symmetry of order 3?

Activity Sheet 8.3

Activity 8.3

Regular polygons have an order of rotational symmetry equal to their number of sides.

Discussion 8.3

What does quadrant mean? What is different about the co-ordinate system shown compared to the basic first quadrant system?

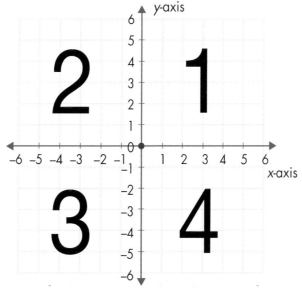

What are the co-ordinates of the origin?

The quadrant labelled 1 is the first quadrant and all points in this quadrant will have positive x and y co-ordinates.

Copy and complete the table.

Quadrant	Point in quadrant	Statement about points in quadrant
1	(2, 3)	positive x and y co-ordinates
2		
3		
4		

Identify the quadrant that each point lies in: (2, –4), (–2, 5), (2, 1), (–3, –4).

Name a point which lies between quadrants 1 and 2.

Between which two quadrants does the point (–3, 0) lie?

Name a point which lies between quadrants 1 and 4.

Between which two quadrants does the point (0, –3) lie?

State some points that lie on the x-axis. What is similar about each of these points?

Exercise 8b

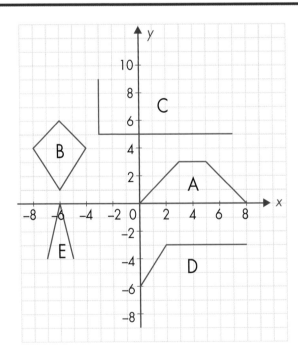

1 a i Write down the co-ordinates of the vertices of shape A.

   ii What is the name of this quadrilateral?

   b i Write down the co-ordinates of the vertices of shape B.

   ii What is the name of this quadrilateral?

c Three vertices of a rectangle, labelled C, are shown. What are the co-ordinates of the final vertex?

d Three vertices of a parallelogram, labelled D, are shown. What are the co-ordinates of the final vertex?

e Three vertices of a rhombus labelled E, are shown. What are the co-ordinates of the final vertex?

2 a Draw a set of co-ordinate axes that range from −8 to 8 on both axes.

b i Plot and join the following points in order to make a triangle.

(0, 5) (5, 5) (0, 7) (0, 5)

ii What type of triangle have you plotted?

c i Plot and join the following points in order to make a quadrilateral.

(0, 0) (−5, 2) (−4, 0) (−5, −2) (0, 0)

ii What is the name of this quadrilateral?

iii How many lines of symmetry has this shape?

d i Plot and join the following points in order to make a quadrilateral.

(−3, −3) (−3, −7) (−1, −6) (−1, −3) (−3, −3)

ii What is the name of this quadrilateral?

iii Join (0, −3) to (0, −7) and draw the reflection of your quadrilateral in this line.

iv List the co-ordinates of the vertices of this reflection.

e i Plot and join the following points in order: (−1, 4) (−6, 4) (−6, 7).

ii Complete the rectangle and write down the co-ordinates of the final vertex.

iii Rule on the diagonals and list the co-ordinates of the point of intersection.

f i Plot and join the following points in order to make a polygon:

(4, 1) (4, 2) (8, 3) (8, 0) (6, 2) (5, 1) (4, 1)

ii Name the polygon.

iii Rule a dotted line from (4, −2) to (8, −2).

iv Reflect your polygon in the dotted line and list the co-ordinates of the vertices.

g i Two of the vertices of an isosceles triangle are located at (−8, 5) and (−5, 0). Plot and join these points.

ii The third vertex lies in the third quadrant. What is its location? Plot this vertex and complete the triangle.

h Join (–3, 2) to (3, 2) with a straight line. What are the co-ordinates of the mid-point of this line?

i Join (6, 4) to (8, 6). If this line is a diagonal of a square, draw the square and list the co-ordinates of the other two vertices.

Activity 8.4

Activity
Sheet 8.4

Activity 8.5

Activity
Sheet 8.5

Activity 8.6

Activity
Sheet 8.6

Discussion 8.4

The diagram shows a pattern of tessellating rectangles. Are all the rectangles congruent? Each rectangle is 3 cm long and 1 cm wide. Describe the movement from the pink rectangle in the top left of the pattern to the next pink rectangle on the top row. Describe the movement from the pink rectangle in the top left of the pattern to the pink rectangle in the right of the pattern on the bottom row. Describe how to move from the final yellow rectangle on the bottom row to the first yellow rectangle on the top row.

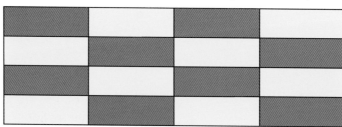

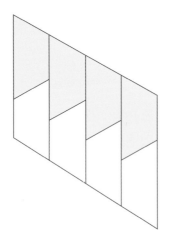

These movements are called **translations**. A translation 'slides' an **object** a fixed distance in a given direction. The result of the translation is called an **image**. The original object and its translated image are **congruent.** Translations are always given with the horizontal shift in movement listed first and the vertical shift second.

In this tessellating pattern are the yellow tiles translations? Are the white tiles translations? Can a yellow tile be translated to the location of a white tile?

Can you think of any 'real-life' translations?

Exercise 8c

1 a Object A has been translated to Image B. Describe the translation.

b Have all vertices moved the same distance in the same direction?

c Describe the translation required to move B back to A.

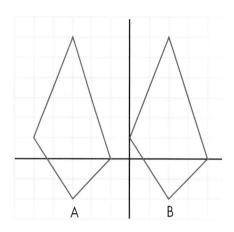

A   B

2 a Object A has been translated to Image B. Describe the translation.

b Describe the translation required to move B back to A.

c Ann says shape C is a translation of shape B. Do you agree? Explain your answer.

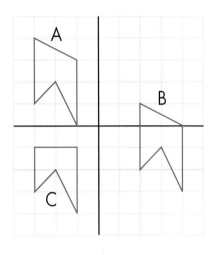

3 a Draw a set of co-ordinate axes ranging from –6 to 6 on both axes.

b Plot and join the points in order to form a quadrilateral. (–6, 2) (–6, 5) (–4, 5) (–3, 2) (–6, 2).

c Name this quadrilateral.

d Translate the quadrilateral 8 units to the right and 5 units down.

e On the same set of axes draw another quadrilateral by plotting and joining these points: (1, 1) (2, 5) (6, 6) (5, 2) (1, 1).

f Name this quadrilateral.

g Translate this quadrilateral 6 units to the left and 7 units down.

h Describe the translation required to get back to the original shape.

4 a Which of these shapes could triangle X map to after a translation?

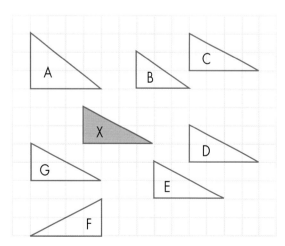

b Describe each of the possible translations.

c Is it possible for two congruent shapes not to be a translation of one another? Explain using the triangles above.

5 a Draw a set of co-ordinate axes ranging from –6 to 6 on both axes.

b Plot and join the points in order to draw a quadrilateral: (2, 2) (2, 4) (6, 3) (4, 1) (2, 2). Label your shape P.

c Translate quadrilateral P, 2 units left and 5 units down. Label this shape Q.

d Write down the co-ordinates of the vertices of Q.

e Translate Q, 5 units left and 6 units up. Label this shape R and list the co-ordinates of the vertices.

f Plot and join the following points in order: (–4, –5) (–4, –3) (0, –4) (–2, –6) (–4, –5). Label this shape S.

g Describe the translation that maps R onto S.

h Describe the translation that maps S onto R.

6 a If a shape is translated 5 units left and 4 units up, then translated again 2 units right and 5 units down, what translation is required to get back to the original?

b If a shape is translated x units across and y units up or down what translation is needed to return to the original location?

Discussion 8.5

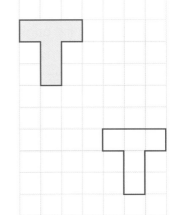

Translations are often described using vectors. The shaded shape T has been translated $\begin{pmatrix} 4 \\ -5 \end{pmatrix}$. What does this mean?

$\begin{pmatrix} 4 \\ -5 \end{pmatrix}$ is an example of a column vector.

What direction does the top part of the column vector refer to? And the bottom? How would a translation of 6 units left and 2 units up be written? What about 3 units right and 3 units down? What translation does the column vector $\begin{pmatrix} -4 \\ 0 \end{pmatrix}$ perform?

Exercise 8d

A

1 **a** Plot the vertices of a shape A as (0, 4), (1, 4), (1, 2) and (0, 3) onto centimetre squared paper. Use co-ordinate axes that range from −10 to 10 on both axes.

   b Translate A $\begin{pmatrix} 2 \\ 2 \end{pmatrix}$ and label it B.

   c Translate A $\begin{pmatrix} -2 \\ 4 \end{pmatrix}$ and label it C.

   d Translate A $\begin{pmatrix} 0 \\ -5 \end{pmatrix}$ and label it D.

   e Translate A $\begin{pmatrix} -3 \\ -4 \end{pmatrix}$ and label it E.

   What column vector is needed to move from:

   f E back to A?   **g** D to C?   **h** B to C?   **i** E to D?

2 **a** Copy the diagram onto squared paper.

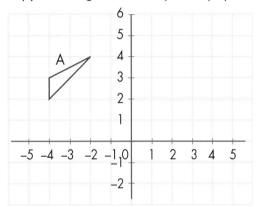

   b Translate A $\begin{pmatrix} 4 \\ -2 \end{pmatrix}$ and label the new shape B.

   c What vector translates B back to A?

   d Translate B $\begin{pmatrix} 3 \\ 5 \end{pmatrix}$ and label the new shape C.

   What vector translates:

   e C back to B?   **f** A to C?   **g** C to A?

   h What rule connects a vector translating A to B with its reverse, which translates B back to A?

   i Use your diagram and answers so far to investigate the relationship between the vectors for the translation A to C with the vectors for the translations A to B and then to C. Summarise your findings.

3 The point A (3, 4) is translated $\begin{pmatrix} 3 \\ 5 \end{pmatrix}$. What is the point's new location?

4 The point A (−2, 0) is translated $\begin{pmatrix} 1 \\ -4 \end{pmatrix}$. What is the point's new location?

5 The point A (−3, 6) is translated 4 units up and 2 units to the left. What is its new location?

Discussion 8.6

Translations are one type of **transformation**. **Reflections** are also transformations. Look at the shapes here which have been reflected in the mirror line.

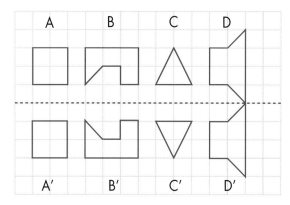

Describe the position of each transformed image in relation to its object. One of the objects has a vertex on the mirror line. What happens to this vertex when it is reflected?

Activity Sheet 8.7

Activity 8.7

Example 8.1

Mirror lines can also be diagonal. Reflect the shape in the given mirror line.

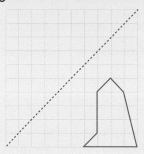 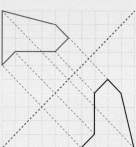

Exercise 8e

SUS8e

1   Reflect the shapes in the mirror lines.

 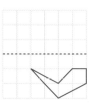   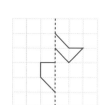

2 a Reflect triangle *ABC* in the *x*-axis and write down the new co-ordinates of *A*, *B* and *C*.

b Reflect triangle *ABC* in the *y*-axis and write down the new co-ordinates of of *A*, *B* and *C*.

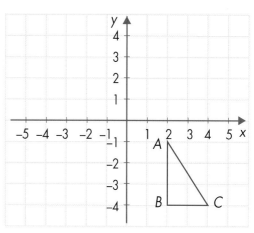

3 Reflect the shapes in the given mirror lines.

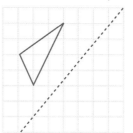 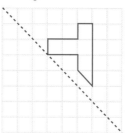 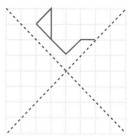

4 Some reflections are shown. Copy the diagrams and draw on the mirror lines.

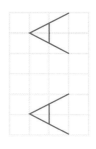 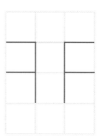 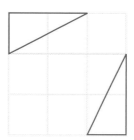 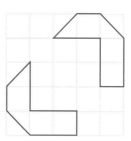

Discussion 8.7

A famous Hungarian mathematician Lipót Fejér was born in this house in the city of Pécs (in the south of Hungary) in 1880. What is the problem with this photo? A larger version of the same photo is now shown.

This is an example of another type of transformation, called an **enlargement**. How many times longer is the larger image than the original object? How many times wider is the image than the object? Each dimension has been multiplied by 3 so the **scale factor** is 3. What would the dimensions of the picture be if the original was enlarged by a scale factor of 10?

A shape is enlarged by a scale factor of 4. If the original length is 6 cm, what length is the enlarged image? The height of the enlarged image is 16 cm. What height is the object? Where would you see enlargements in real life?

Exercise 8f

1 Copy these shapes onto squared paper. Enlarge each shape using the given scale factor.

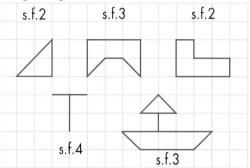

2 a Copy the diagram onto squared paper.

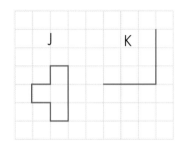

b Shape K is where James has started to draw the enlargement of Shape J. Complete shape K.

c What is the scale factor of the enlargement?

3 The picture of the car has been enlarged as shown.

0.7 m

1.5 m
original

3 m
enlargement

A

a What is the missing length, A?

b What is the scale factor of the enlargement?

4 Jenny finds the following paper sizes diagram (drawn to scale) on the internet.

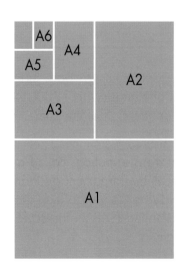

a If A6 is the object what paper size is an enlargement of

  i scale factor 2?

  ii scale factor 4?

b If the dimensions of a sheet of A5 paper are 148 mm by 210 mm, what are the dimensions of

  i a sheet of A3 paper?

  ii a sheet of A1 paper?

5 A kite with diagonals 6 cm and 2 cm has a pair of equal interior angles of size 140°. The kite is enlarged so that the diagonals now measure 18 cm and 6 cm.

a What is the scale factor of the enlargement?

b What size are the equal interior angles of the enlarged image?

Discussion 8.8

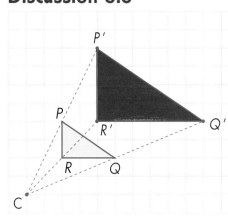

Sometimes the position of an enlargement is important. In this case a **centre of enlargement** will be given. The yellow triangle *PQR* has been enlarged about the centre *C*. The resulting image *P'Q'R'* is shown in pink. What is the scale factor of the enlargement? The dashed lines are called **rays** or **construction lines**. How many rays have been drawn? Why do you think this number has been drawn? Rays are always drawn from the centre of enlargement through each vertex of the object in a straight line. The length of a ray is simply the length from the centre to each vertex multiplied by the scale factor. When the ends of the rays (*P'*, *Q'* and *R'*) are joined together the result is the enlarged image.

Exercise 8g

SUS8g

1   Use SUS8g. Enlarge the shape *JKLM* by scale factor 2 about the centre *O* by following the given instructions.

Step 1: Copy the diagram onto squared paper.

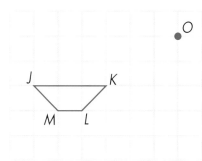

Step 2: Measure the length of *OK* and multiply this length by the scale factor. Draw a ray this length with dashed lines from *O* through *K* and label the image point *K'* as shown.

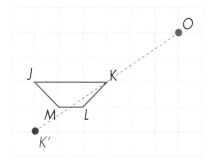

Step 3: Repeat this procedure with the other three vertices as shown.

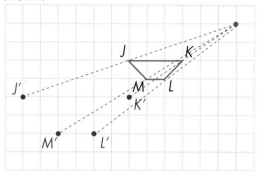

Step 4: Finally join the points in order as shown.

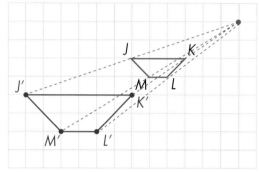

Step 5: Check each length has been doubled on the image.

2 Shape *ABCD* has been enlarged about *O*. What is the scale factor of the enlargement?

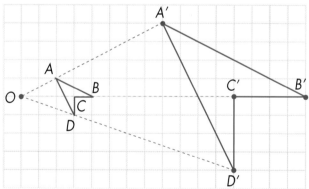

3 **a** Draw a pair of co-ordinate axes that range from 0 to 10 on each axis.

   b Plot the following points and join them in order: (1, 2) (2, 2) (3, 3) (1, 3) (1, 2).

   c What type of quadrilateral have you plotted?

   d Enlarge this shape by a scale factor of 3 about the origin.

   e List the co-ordinates of the vertices of the image.

   f What link can you find between the co-ordinates of the subject and those of the enlarged image?

4 For each of the parts of this question use a new page of squared paper and copy the diagrams, then draw the enlargements centred on *O* using the given scale factor.

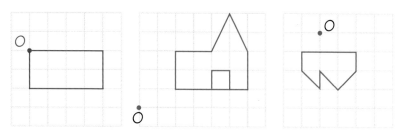

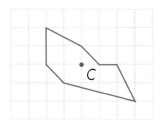

a scale factor 3   **b** scale factor 2   **c** scale factor 3

5 Copy this shape and enlarge it about C using a scale factor of 3.

Example 8.2

Object A has been enlarged to image B. Find the centre of enlargement.

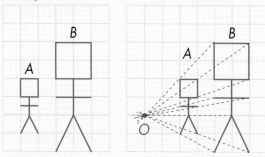

Join the image vertices to their corresponding vertices on the object and extend all lines until they meet. Where the lines meet (marked O) is the centre of enlargement.

Exercise 8h

SUS8h

1 a Copy the following shapes onto squared paper and find the centre of enlargement.

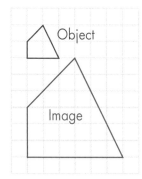
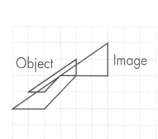
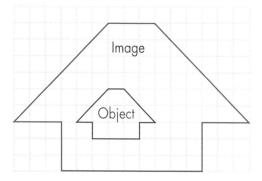

b State the scale factor for each of the enlargements.

Activity 8.9

Activity
Sheet 8.9

Consolidation Exercise

1   James says the cloud to the right has rotational symmetry of order 1. Julie says it has no rotational symmetry. Who is correct? Explain your answer.

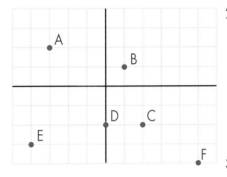

2   Write down the column vectors for the translations given on the left.

   a A to B   **b** A to C   **c** A to D   **d** A to E   **e** A to F

   f B to A   **g** B to E   **h** B to F   **i** C to D   **j** C to E

   k D to A   **l** D to C   **m** E to A   **n** E to F   **o** F to A

   p F to B

3   Draw a set of co-ordinate axes ranging from –6 to 6 on both axes.

   a Plot the points A (1, 2), B (3, 3) and C (5, 2)

   b Write down the co-ordinates of point D, so that ABCD is a rhombus.

   c Join the points to draw the rhombus.

   d The rhombus is translated so that vertex A moves to (–5, –3). Draw the rhombus in its translated position.

   e Write down the column vector of this translation.

   f Write down the co-ordinates of the mid-point of the original rhombus.

   g Translate this mid-point using the column vector found in part **e** and write down the co-ordinates of its new location. Is your answer as expected?

4   Is B a translation of A? Explain your answer.

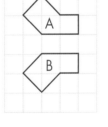

5   Draw an enlargement of the shape, centred at C, with scale factor **i** 2 **ii** 3.

9 The circle

Discussion 9.1

In everyday life people use shapes to express their feelings. Have you ever heard the expression 'I feel like I am running around in circles'? What does this mean?

What other meaning can going around in circles conjure up?

In mathematics a **circle** refers to a shape with all points the same distance from the **centre**.

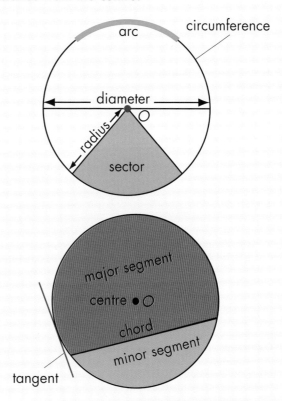

Exercise 9a

1 Use the information in the box to match each circle part to its correct definition and picture.

Circle	The larger section of a circle divided by a chord	
Tangent	The smaller section of a circle divided by a chord	
Centre	A line segment within a circle that touches two points on the circle	
Arc	The longest line segment that touches two points on the circle, passing through the centre	
Semi-circle	A circle wedge	
Circumference	The distance from the centre of the circle to any point on the circumference	
Radius	Half of a circle	
Major segment	A shape whose points are all equidistant from a central point	
Sector	The centre of the circle	
Chord	A curved line that is part of the circumference of a circle	
Diameter	A line perpendicular to the radius that touches only one point on the circumference	
Minor segment	The perimeter of the circle	

2 In each of the pictures name the part of a circle which is shown in black.

a

b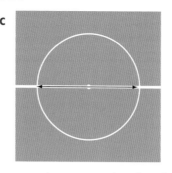

c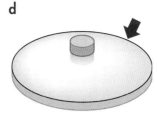

d

3 Use compasses to draw a circle of radius 5 cm.

   a Draw a radius in the circle and label it.

   b Draw a chord and label it.

   c Label the circumference.

   d Measure the diameter of the circle.

   e How does the length of the diameter compare with the radius? Will this be the case for every circle?

4 A circle has a diameter of 12 cm.

   a What length will the radius of this circle be?

   b Use compasses to draw the circle. Label the centre of the circle O. Measure the radius to check if your answer to **a** is correct.

   c Draw any two radii and label them OA and OB.

   d Draw the line AB and label it.

   e Copy and complete the sentence:

     The line AB divides the circle into two _____; a _____ segment and a _____ segment.

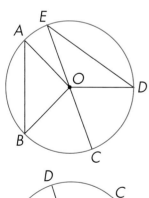

5 Look at the diagram and answer the questions. O is the centre of the circle.

   a How many radii are drawn? Name them.

   b Name two chords.

   c What is the mathematical name for EC?

   d What types of triangles are AOB and DOE? Give a reason to support your answer.

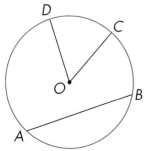

6 Make a copy of the diagram. O is the centre of the circle.

   a On your diagram draw over the arc AB in blue.

   b Label the minor segment.

   c Draw around a sector in red and label it.

   d Add a tangent to the diagram.

Activity
Sheet 9.1

Activity 9.1

Discussion 9.2

In ancient times the circle was sometimes used as a basic plan in buildings. Do you know where there is a round tower in Northern Ireland? Why were towers built in **circular** form?

In P.E. John has to run around a circular track. He wants to calculate the total length he has to run in one complete circuit. He tries to measure the distance around the edge using a tape. However, he has a problem keeping the tape on the curved edges. His teacher tells him if he measures the diameter of each circle he will then be able to calculate the distance around the track, or circumference, using a formula involving pi.

The symbol for pi is π. The teacher explains that π **is the ratio of the circumference of a circle to its diameter.**

John does not understand what the teacher means and so she sets the class an activity to help them understand.

Activity
Sheet 9.2

Activity 9.2

The Egyptians and the Babylonians were the earliest civilisations to use π. Two thousand years ago π was taken to be 3. Although the value was close, as time passed efforts were made to refine the ratio to a more precise number. The Greek mathematician, Archimedes, stated that it fell between $3\frac{10}{70}$, and $3\frac{10}{71}$. In the computer age, the number has been calculated to one million decimal places.

Activity
Sheet 9.3

Activity 9.3

Discussion 9.3

π may be approximated to different values but it is often taken as 3.14 to two decimal places. How will this help John to find the circumference of the running track?

The circumference or perimeter of any circle can be found by multiplying the diameter by π.

C = π d

where C is the circumference and d is the diameter.

Since the diameter is twice the radius **r**, the formula can also be written as **C = 2πr**

The diameter of the running track is 33 m

C = π × d = 3.14 × 33 m

C = 103.62 m

The distance John runs around the track is 103.62 m correct to 2 decimal places.

Exercise 9b

In Questions **1** to **6**, find the circumference of each of the objects, taking π as 3.14. Round each answer to 2 decimal places.

1
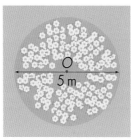
5 m

2
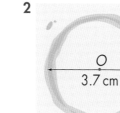
3.7 cm

3
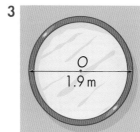
1.9 m

4
7.3 cm

5
0.75 m

6
6 cm

7 In a race, Dave runs around the edge of the inner track and Jane runs around the outside edge of the track. How much further has Jane to run than Dave?

8 Work out the answers in Questions **1** to **7** again. This time use the π button on the calculator. Round the answers to 2 decimal places. Are both sets of answers similar?

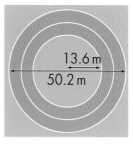
13.6 m
50.2 m

Discussion 9.4

The circumference of a circle is 47.1 cm. How can I find the diameter of this circle? What is the radius of this circle?

By rearranging the formulae it is possible to find the diameter and the radius of a circle if the circumference is known.

$C = \pi d$ so $d = C \div \pi$ similarly $C = 2\pi r$ so $r = C \div 2\pi$

Exercise 9c

Copy and complete the table by finding the missing values. Take π as 3.14 or use the π button on the calculator. Give answers to three significant figures where appropriate.

	Circumference	Diameter	Radius
1	314 m		
2	176 cm		
3	376.8 cm		
4	56.52 ft		
5	94.2 m		
6		13 cm	
7			4 m
8		7.6 m	
9		120 mm	
10			3.25 cm

Discussion 9.5

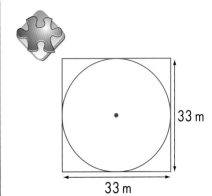

33 m

33 m

The maths teacher has asked John if he could work out the approximate area of the circular running track. John reckons that a good way to find the area of the circle is to use a shape he already knows how to find the area of: the square.

Area of square = 33^2 = 1089 m²

John shows the teacher his method and explains that an approximate area of the running track is 1089 m².

Do you think this is a good idea? Can you suggest a more accurate method which John could use?

Activity 9.4

The area of a circle can be found accurately by using a formula.

$A = \pi r^2$

where **A** is the area and **r** is the radius of the circle.

To find the area of the running track:

$d = 33\,\text{m}$

$\text{radius} = d \div 2 = 33 \div 2 = 16.5\,\text{m}$

$\text{area of circle} = \pi r^2$

$\qquad\qquad\quad = \pi \times 16.5^2\,\text{m}^2$

$\qquad\qquad\quad = 855.2985999\,\text{m}^2$

$\qquad\qquad\quad = 855.3\,\text{m}^2\,(1\,\text{d.p.})$

Note that the calculator button for x^2 has been used in this calculation.

Exercise 9d

In questions **1** to **6**, calculate the area of each of the circles. Take π as 3.14 or use the π button on the calculator. Give answers to three significant figures where appropriate.

1

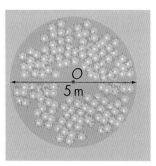

O
$5\,\text{m}$

2

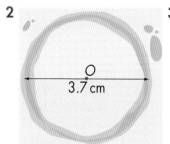

O
$3.7\,\text{cm}$

3

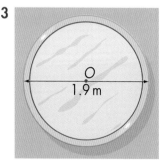

O
$1.9\,\text{m}$

4

O
$7.3\,\text{cm}$

BEANS

5

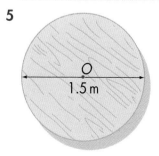

O
$1.5\,\text{m}$

6

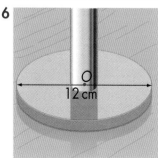

O
$12\,\text{cm}$

7 Navan Fort is a circular site which is 240 m in diameter. Find the area of the base of the fort in square metres.

8 The PE teacher has drawn two separate circles on the floor of the gym. The smaller circle has a diameter of 5.2 m and the larger circle has a diameter of 8.5 m.

 a Find the distance around the perimeter of each shape.

 b What is the total area enclosed inside both circles?

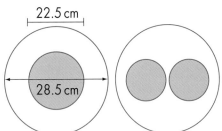

22.5 cm

28.5 cm

b   c

9 Plates come in different sizes and are sized according to the diameter.

 It is possible to buy four different sizes of plates:

 saucer 140 mm, side plate 15 cm, salad plate 22.5 cm, dinner plate 28.5 cm.

 a What is the difference in area between the saucer and the side plate?

 b Harry uses a dinner plate as a template to cut out a large circle on a piece of card. He draws a smaller circle inside the larger one using a salad plate. He then cuts out the smaller circle. What area of card is left?

 c Rob cuts out a white circle, the size of a dinner plate. He then places two saucers side by size on top of the white circle. What area of the white circle remains uncovered?

10 A 5-litre circular-based pedal bin has a diameter of 20 cm and a 30-litre pedal bin has a diameter of 30 cm. Calculate the difference in the area of floor space taken up by the bins.

Discussion 9.6

If the area of the circle is given, how can I work out the diameter?

Example 9.1

The area of a chocolate coin is 50.24 cm^2. Find the diameter of the coin.

Since $A = \pi r^2$

$50.24 = \pi \times r^2$

$50.24 \div \pi = r^2$

$16 = r^2$ (Taking π as 3.14)

$\sqrt{16} = r$

$4 = r$

Since the radius of the coin is 4 cm, the diameter is $4 \times 2 = 8$ cm

Exercise 9e

In each of the questions, round the answer to an appropriate degree of accuracy.

1 The area of a circular table is $5.47 \, m^2$. What is its diameter?

2 A child's hula hoop has an area of $615.44 \, inches^2$. Find the radius of the hoop.

3 A button has an area of $12.56 \, cm^2$. What is the diameter of the button?

4 A mini roundabout has an area of $63.585 \, m^2$. What is the radius of the roundabout?

5 The circular base of a jam jar has an area of $3846.5 \, mm^2$. What is the radius of the jar?

Exercise 9f

1 A manufacturer makes circular tablecloths. To calculate the area of material required they ask the customer for the exact measurement of the table's diameter. In addition they allow 30 cm for the drape to hang over the edges of the table.

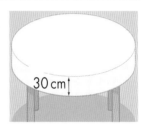

30 cm

a How much greater than the diameter of the table is the diameter of the tablecloth?

b Calculate the area of material needed, in m^2, for each of the orders. Give the answers correct to two decimal places.

Each tablecloth is cut from a square whose side length is equal to the diameter of the tablecloth.

c Work out the area of material wasted in each of the three orders.

d The material costs £12.99 per m^2. Calculate the cost of each tablecloth.

Order number	Table diameter
001	214 cm
002	259 cm
003	350 cm

2 Rings in jewellery shops are sized according to diameter measurement. The table shows some of the sizes used.

For each ring size, calculate the circumference of the ring.

3 Tractor wheel sizes are graded according to the overall diameter of the wheel.

The manufacturer claims that the rolling circumference of a wheel of diameter 43.1 inches is 130 inches.

a Is this claim true? Show calculations to support your answer.

b What is the rolling circumference of a tyre with a diameter of 55.9 inches?

Ring size	Measurement (diameter) mm
P	56.25
Q	57.50
R	58.75
S	60.00

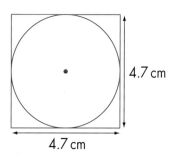

4.7 cm

4.7 cm

4 **a** Harry cuts this circle out of a square piece of paper. What is the diameter of the circle?

b What is the area of the circle?

c What area of paper is wasted?

5 The centre circle on a football pitch has a radius of 9.15 m.

a What is the circumference of the centre circle?

b What area is enclosed within the circle?

6 On a mini hockey pitch the shooting circle has a radius of 14.63 m. The circle has to be marked on the pitch using white tape. What length of tape will be needed?

7 The front wheel of the Penny Farthing bicycle had a diameter of 1.5 m.

a How far did the bicycle travel in one revolution of the front wheel?

b How many revolutions of the wheel are needed to travel a distance of 5 km?

Consolidation Exercise

1 The Big Wheel in Belfast has a radius of 30 m.

How far will one of the cars move in one complete turn of the wheel? Give the answer correct to one decimal place.

2 A circular patio has an area of 78.5 m².

a Find the radius of the patio.

b Paddy wishes to put a wooden edging around the outside of the patio. What length of edging will he need to order?

c Edging costs £4.95 per metre. How much will it cost to do this?

26 inches

3 Sam has a bicycle with 26-inch alloy rims while his friend has a bicycle with 20-inch alloy wheels.

Calculate how much further Sam will go in 100 complete revolutions of his wheels on his bike than his friend.

4 A basketball backboard and net set has a 46 cm circumference ring.

Find the diameter and internal area of the ring.

5 The rear wheel of a wheelchair is 60 cm in diameter. Dave travels a distance of 1.5 km in his wheelchair. How many turns will the rear wheel have to make to complete this?

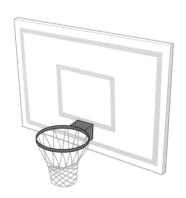

6 Freda's teacher asks her to draw a circle which has an area of 100 square millimetres.

Taking π as 3.14, find out the radius and circumference of Freda's circle. Give the answers correct to three significant figures.

Task 2: Football calendar

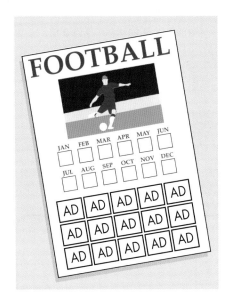

The school football team needs to raise money to go on tour. The coach has suggested that one way of raising the necessary funds is to make a football calendar and ask sponsors to buy advertising space.

● The overall size of the finished calendar is a rectangle measuring 590 mm long by 420 mm wide.

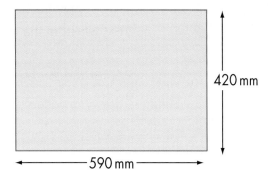

● The photograph of the team measures 265 mm by 160 mm.

● Each advertising space is in the shape of a rectangle measuring 67 mm long by 55 mm wide.

● Each of the 12 calendar months are to be printed in the form of a square of side length 37 mm.

1 Calculate the overall area of the finished calendar.

2 What area of the calendar will be taken up with the team photograph?

3 What total area of the sheet is needed for all the months?

4 What area of the overall calendar will be available for advertising?

5 Work in pairs or as part of a group to design and plan the layout of the school calendar.

6 How many adverts did you manage to position on your calendar layout? If the school decides to sell one advertising space for £15, calculate how much money can be made from the advertising alone.

7 Compare your calendar with other groups in your class. Which layout looks best?

Which layout makes the most money for the school?

10 Sequences and linear graphs

In this chapter, I am learning to:

- find the *n*th term of a linear sequence
- find the *n*th term of a simple quadratic sequence
- draw a linear graph from its equation
- find the equation of a linear graph.

Discussion 10.1

Simon is drawing patterns with dots and lines.

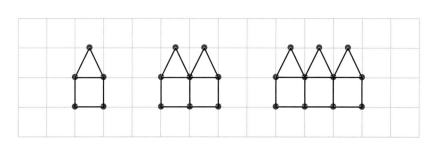

He draws a table to show the number of lines used for different pattern numbers.

Pattern number (*n*)	1	2	3	4	5	6		*n*
Number of lines	6	11	16	21	26			

The number of lines forms a sequence: 6   11   16   21   26 ...

The first term of the sequence is 6, the second term is 11 and so on.

Without drawing the patterns, can you work out the number of lines needed for pattern number 5? What about pattern number 6?

You probably used the difference between terms of the sequence to get your answers. The difference is 5 each time.

$$+5 \quad +5 \quad +5 \quad +5$$
$$6 \quad 11 \quad 16 \quad 21$$

Simon says that he used the difference between the terms to work out that the *n*th term of his sequence is $5n + 1$.

How can you show that Simon's answer is correct?

How did he know to 'add 1' to '$5n$'?

Simon draws another table to show the number of dots used for a different sequence.

Pattern number (n)	1	2	3	4	5	6		n
Number of dots	4	11	18	25				

How would you complete the table?

What is the difference for this sequence?

Use the difference method to work out the *n*th term for this sequence.

Check that your *n*th term is correct by trying out different values of *n*.

What is the pattern number of the diagram that will have 53 dots when this pattern is followed? Explain how you obtained your answer.

Exercise 10a

1 For each of the sequences

   a write down the next two terms, **b** find the *n*th term.

   i 3 5 7 9 11   **ii** 3 7 11 15 19

   iii 1 5 9 13 17   **iv** 2 7 12 17 22

   v 8 11 14 17 20   **vi** 2 8 14 20 26

   vii 10 30 50 70 90   **viii** –15 –10 –5 0 5

   ix 18 15 12 9 6

2 Helena is drawing patterns with trapezia.

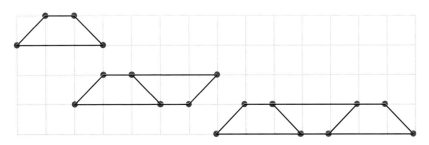

   She draws a table to show the number of lines used for different numbers of trapezia.

Number of trapezia (n)	1	2	3	4	5	6
Number of lines	4	7	10			

a Copy and complete the table.

b Find the *n*th term of the sequence.

c Use the *n*th term to calculate how many lines would be needed when 17 trapezia are used in the pattern.

d Helena uses 46 lines for one pattern. How many trapezia did she draw?

3 Beth is making patterns with black and white tiles.

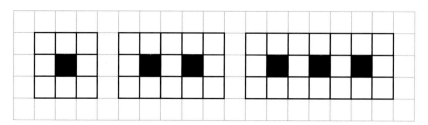

She draws a table to show how many white tiles are needed for different numbers of black tiles.

Number of black tiles	1	2	3	4	5	6
Number of white tiles	8	13	18			

a Copy and complete the table without drawing the patterns.

b Find the *n*th term of the sequence for the white tiles.

c Use the *n*th term to calculate how many white tiles would be needed if 10 black tiles are used in the pattern.

d How many black tiles would be used in a pattern which has 63 white tiles?

Discussion 10.2

Eimear wants to find the *n*th term of this sequence.

3   6   11   18   27 ...

She knows that the difference between terms can help to find the *n*th term so she writes down the difference between the terms of this sequence.

3   6   11   18   27

+ 3   + 5   + 7   + 9

What are the next two terms in this sequence?

What can you say about the difference between the terms?

Eimear says that because the differences are not the same, she cannot use them work out the *n*th term. Instead she then works out the **second difference.**

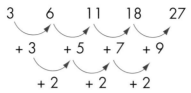

What can you say about the second differences?

If the first difference between the terms of a sequence is constant (the same each time) then the sequence is **linear** and involves terms in *n*.

If the second difference for a sequence is constant, the sequence is **quadratic** and the *n*th term will involve an n^2 term. If the second difference is 2 then the *n*th term of the sequence will have $(1)n^2$.

Eimear makes out a table for the sequence including values for n^2.

Term number (*n*)	1	2	3	4	5
Term value	3	6	11	18	27
n^2	1	4	9	16	25

Can you write down the *n*th term for Eimear's sequence?

Exercise 10b

1 The first five terms of a sequence are:

0   3   8   15   24 ...

a Copy the sequence and write down the first difference. What do you notice?

b Write down the second difference. What do you notice?

c Copy and complete the table for the sequence.

Term number (*n*)	1	2	3	4	5
Term value					
n^2					

d Write down the *n*th term of the sequence.

e What is the 15th term?

f One of the terms is 99. Which term is this?

2 The first five terms of a sequence are:

11   14   19   26   35 ...

a Copy the sequence and write down the first difference. What do you notice?

b Write down the second difference. What do you notice?

c Complete the table for the sequence.

Term number (n)	1	2	3	4	5
Term value					
n^2					

d Write down the nth term of the sequence.

e What is the 15th term?

f One of the terms is 91. Which term is this?

3 Find the nth term for these sequences. Set your work out as in questions **1** and **2**.

    a 4   7   12   19 ...

    b −1   2   7   14 ...

    c −1   −4   −9   −16 ...

    d 6   9   14   21 ...

Discussion 10.3

Look at the function machine.

The values from the function machine can be used as co-ordinates to plot points on a grid.

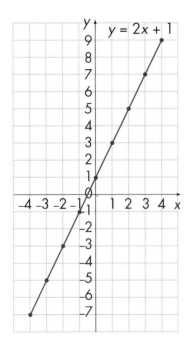

Input x	$2x + 1$	Output y
0		1
1		3
2		5
3		7

The points can be joined to give a straight line.

Give the coordinates of another point on this line.

Is the point (1.5, 4) on this line?

We can say that the **equation** of this line is $y = 2x + 1$.

We usually use a table for the x co-ordinates and their corresponding y co-ordinates rather than using a function machine.

Copy and complete the table for the points on this line.

x co-ordinate	0	1		
y co-ordinate	1			

The equation of a straight line is a rule connecting the x and y co-ordinates of every point on that line. We can find the y co-ordinate at any point on the line if we know the x co-ordinate and the equation of the line.

Exercise 10c

1   Follow these instructions to draw the line with equation $y = 2x - 1$.

   a   Copy and complete the function machine.

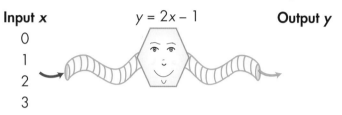

| Input x | $y = 2x - 1$ | Output y |

Input x: 0, 1, 2, 3

   b   Copy and complete the table using the values from your function machine.

x co-ordinate	0	1	2	3
y co-ordinate				

   c   Draw axes from −5 to +5 and plot these points. Join the points with a straight line. This is the line with equation $y = 2x - 1$. Label the line with its equation.

   d   Copy and complete the following sentence.

   If this line were extended, the point (100, ____) would lie on it.

2   Follow these instructions to draw the line $y = x + 1$.

   a   Copy and complete the table by substituting the x co-ordinate values into the equation to find the y co-ordinates.

x co-ordinate	−1	0	1	2
y co-ordinate				

   b   Draw axes from −4 to +4 and plot these points. Join the points with a straight line. This is the line with equation $y = x + 1$. Label the line with its equation.

3   Use these instructions to help you to draw the line $y = 2x + 2$.

   a   Copy and complete the table.

x co-ordinate	−1	0	1	2
y co-ordinate				

   b   Draw axes from −4 to +6 and plot these points. Join the points with a straight line. This is the line with equation $y = 2x + 2$. Label the line with its equation.

c Write down the coordinates of two other points on the line $y = 2x + 2$.

4 Use these instructions to help you to draw the line $y = 5 - 2x$.

a Copy and complete the table.

x co-ordinate	−1	0	1	2
y co-ordinate				

b Use the table to draw the line $y = 5 - 2x$. Use suitable axes.

c Write down the co-ordinates of two other points on the line $y = 5 - 2x$.

d Write down what you notice about this line compared to the others so far. What is different about the equation of this line?

Activity 10.1

Activity
Sheet 10.1

Discussion 10.4

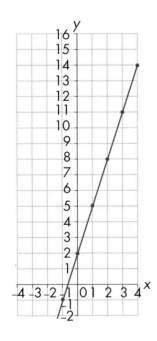

Scott wants to find the equation of the line drawn on the grid.

He knows that the equation of a line is a rule connecting the x and y co-ordinates of the points on the line. He wants to find out what this rule is.

He starts by drawing a table to show the co-ordinates.

x co-ordinate	−1	0	1	2	3
y co-ordinate	−1	2			

What should Scott put in the empty boxes?

What pattern do you see in the y co-ordinate row of the table?

What do you need to do to the x co-ordinate each time to get the y co-ordinate?

Write down the equation of the line.

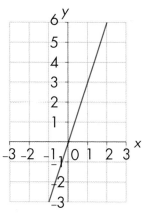

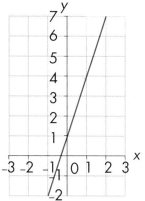

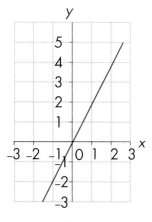

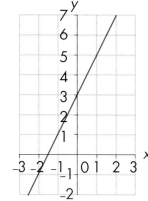

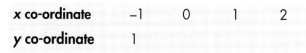

Exercise 10d

For each of the diagrams:

a Copy and complete the table.

b Write down the equation of the line.

1

x co-ordinate	−1	0	1	2
y co-ordinate	−3	0		

2

x co-ordinate	−1	0	1	2
y co-ordinate	−2	1		

3

x co-ordinate	−1	0	1	2
y co-ordinate	−2	0		

4

x co-ordinate	−1	0	1	2
y co-ordinate	1			

5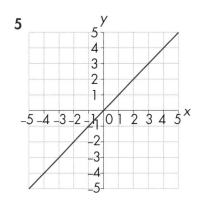

x co-ordinate	–1	0	1	2
y co-ordinate	–1			

Activity
Sheet 10.2

Activity 10.2

Consolidation Exercise

1 Find the *n*th term of these sequences.

a	4	8	12	16	20 ...
b	–4	–8	–12	–16	–20 ...
c	6	11	16	21	26 ...
d	10	5	0	–5	–10 ...
e	7	10	15	22	31 ...
f	–9	–6	–1	6	15 ...
g	99	96	91	84	75 ...

2 John is making patterns using matchsticks.

a Copy and complete the table.

Pattern number (*p*)	1	2	3	4
Number of matchsticks (*m*)				

b Find the *n*th term of the sequence.

c How many matchsticks would be needed to make the 20th pattern in this sequence?

d Which pattern in this sequence will require 31 matchsticks?

3 For each equation, copy and complete the table and draw the graph.

x co-ordinate	−1	0	1	2
y co-ordinate				

a $y = 3x + 2$ x axis from −2 to 4; y axis from −2 to 8

b $y = 4x$ x axis from −2 to 4; y axis from −4 to 8

c $y = 2x − 5$ x axis from −2 to 4; y axis from −8 to 2

d $y = 3 − 2x$ x axis from −2 to 4; y axis from −2 to 8

e $y = −4x$ x axis from −2 to 4; y axis from −8 to 4

f $y = 2 − 3x$ x axis from −2 to 4; y axis from −4 to 6

4 For each of the lines in the diagrams, copy and complete this table each time and write down the equation of the line.

x co-ordinate	−1	0	1	2
y co-ordinate				

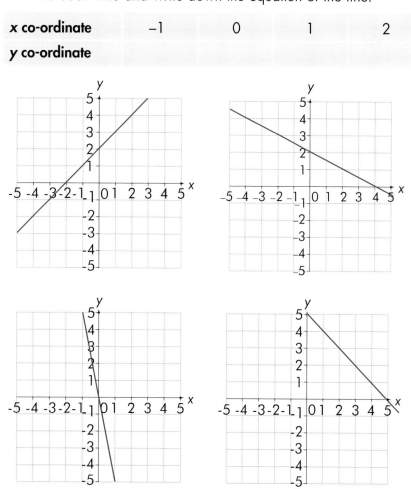

Area and perimeter

Discussion 11.1

Quadro says it is easy to calculate the area of any quadrilateral if you know how to find the area of a rectangle and a triangle. Do you agree with this statement?

Look at the shapes. What type of quadrilateral is each shape? With a partner, suggest a strategy to find their areas. Describe your strategy to the whole class. Which strategy do you think is best for finding their areas? Give a reason for your answer.

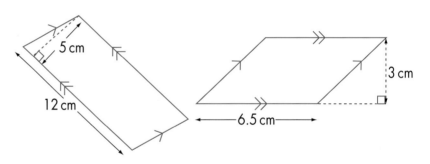

5 cm

12 cm

3 cm

6.5 cm

Resource Activity
Sheet 11.1 Sheet 11.1

Activity 11.1

Area of parallelogram = *bh*

where ***b*** is the base

and ***h*** is the perpendicular height

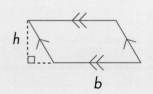

h

b

Exercise 11a

Make sure that you read the units of measurements given in the questions carefully.

1 Calculate the area of each parallelogram. Use the formula and show all calculations clearly. Remember to include the units of area.

a

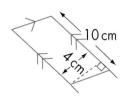

10 cm
4 cm

b

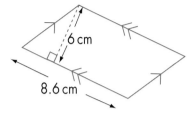

6 cm
8.6 cm

c

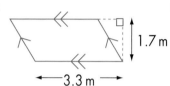

1.7 m
3.3 m

d

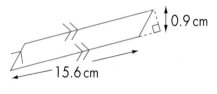

0.9 cm
15.6 cm

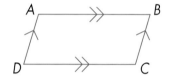

A   B
D   C

2 The area of triangle ADC is 17.6 cm^2.

a What is the area of the parallelogram ABCD?

b Explain how you found the answer.

3 Daniel has been asked by his technology teacher to design a parallelogram shaped paving slab. The area of the slab is to be 400 cm^2. Sketch four possible designs which he could use, marking on the dimensions.

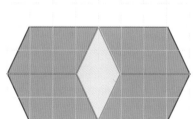

4 Rory makes the mathematical pattern shown on 1 centimetre squared paper. He says that the area of his pattern is 32 cm^2. Show calculations to check if he is correct.

5 Road signs and markings often use parallelograms.

a The blue arrow is made up from two congruent parallelograms. Calculate the area of the arrow in the road sign.

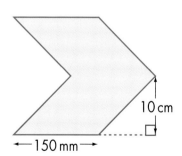

10 cm
←150 mm→

b The diagram shows chevrons marked on a road. Calculate the area of one of the parallelograms in the white chevron.

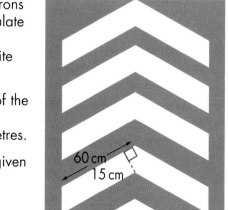

60 cm
15 cm

c Calculate the total area of the white chevrons. Give the answer in square centimetres.

d Change the dimensions given on the diagram of the chevrons to metres.

e Write the total area enclosed within the chevrons in m^2.

6 a Calculate the total area of the road sign in cm².

b Calculate the area of the yellow arrow.

c Calculate the total area of the black triangles.

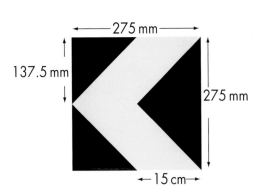

Discussion 11.2

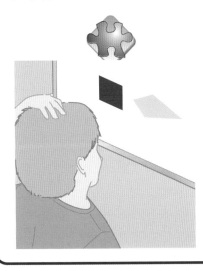

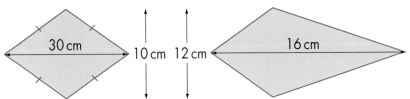

Quadro's teacher has given him two different quadrilaterals and asked him to find the areas. Name each of the quadrilaterals. Suggest a strategy that Quadro can use to find the area of each quadrilateral.

Resource   Activity
Sheet 11.2 Sheet 11.2

Activity 11.2

We can use a formula to find the area of a kite or a rhombus

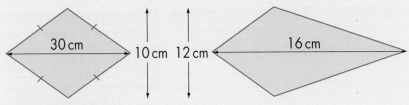

Area of rhombus
= ½ product of the diagonals

Area of kite
= ½ product of the diagonals

Area of rhombus or kite = ½ *ab* where *a* and *b* are the lengths of the diagonals

Example 11.1

Find the area of this kite.

Area of kite = $\frac{1}{2}$ × product of diagonals

$\qquad = \frac{1}{2} \times 30 \times 15$

$\qquad = 225 \text{ cm}^2$

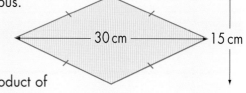

Example 11.2

Find the area of this rhombus.

Area of rhombus = $\frac{1}{2}$ × product of diagonals

$\qquad = \frac{1}{2} \times 30 \text{ cm} \times 15 \text{ cm}$

$\qquad = 225 \text{ cm}^2$

Exercise 11b

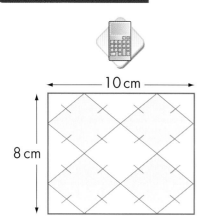

1 Victor makes a kite with diagonals of length 60 cm and 90 cm respectively. What area of material will be needed to fit in the frame exactly?

2 Jackie is making a patchwork quilt cover and she places a pattern in the centre of each of the rectangles.

All the rhombuses in the rectangular shape are congruent.

a Find the length of the diagonals of each rhombus.

b What area of the rectangle is taken up by the four yellow rhombuses?

3 Leonard draws a geometric mosaic pattern in art using 1 centimetre-squared paper.

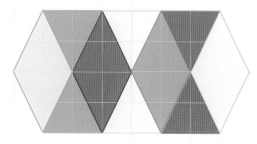

a What area of the pattern is red?

b Calculate the area of the complete mosaic.

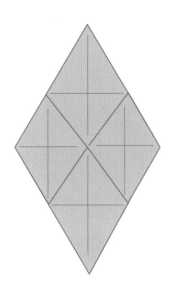

4 Four congruent kites are placed together in a tessellation.

   a What quadrilateral do they form? Give a reason for your answer.

   b The longer diagonal of the kite is 20 cm long and the shorter diagonal is 17 cm long. Calculate the total area of the pattern in the tessellation.

5 Georgina buys a decorated tile when she is on holiday in Turkey.

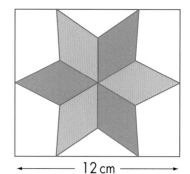

   a If the tile is 12 cm wide, what is the length of the longer diagonal in the rhombus pattern?

   b The shorter diagonal of the rhombus is 3.5 cm. Calculate the area of the tile which is coloured.

12 cm

Discussion 11.3

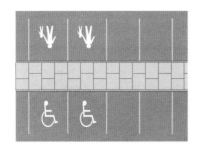

Name the quadrilaterals in the picture.

Where are spaces for disabled parking usually positioned in supermarket car parks? What are the differences between an ordinary parking space and a disabled parking space?

Exercise 11c

Calculate the area of each shape.

1

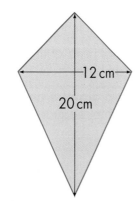

12 cm

20 cm

2

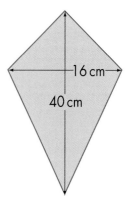

16 cm

40 cm

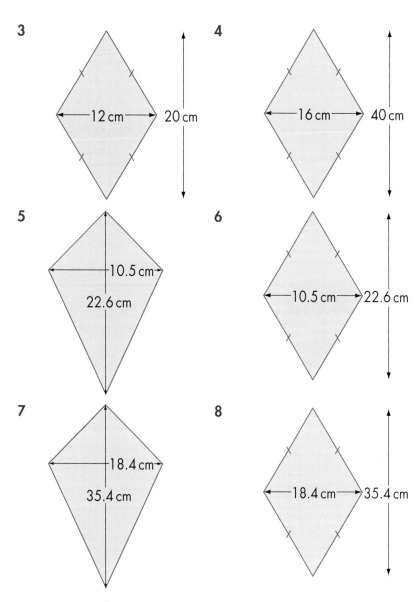

3 12 cm 20 cm

4 16 cm 40 cm

5 10.5 cm 22.6 cm

6 10.5 cm 22.6 cm

7 18.4 cm 35.4 cm

8 18.4 cm 35.4 cm

9 Compare the answers in Questions **1** to **8**. What do you notice?

Discussion 11.4

Name this quadrilateral. Quadro wants to find the area of this quadrilateral. Describe a strategy that he could use.

Quadro's teacher draws him a different trapezium and asks him to find the area.

Do you see any difficulties that he might have when finding the area of this shape?

Activity
Sheet 11.3

Activity 11.3

Area of trapezium $= \frac{1}{2}(a + b)h$

Where a and b are the lengths of the parallel sides

and h is the perpendicular height.

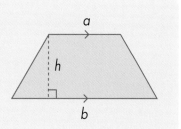

Exercise 11d

1   Calculate the area of each shape, showing clear working. Choose an appropriate unit of area for your answer.

a

3.2 cm

5 cm

7.8 cm

b

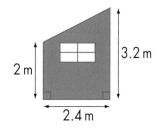

2 m

3.2 m

2.4 m

c

8.8 m

2.9 m

12 m

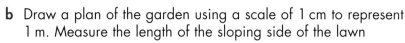

2   Dora's lawn is shown in the diagram.

a Calculate the area of the lawn

b Draw a plan of the garden using a scale of 1 cm to represent 1 m. Measure the length of the sloping side of the lawn

c Use the answer obtained in part **b** to calculate the length of fencing required to completely enclose the lawn.

d Dora digs a circular flower bed which has a diameter of 160 cm, in the centre of the lawn. What is the area of the flower bed to the nearest square metre?

e What area of the garden remains as lawn?

1200 cm

5.8 m

9.6 m

1200 cm

160 cm

5.8 m

9.6 m

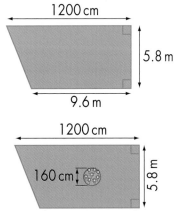

3   In technology class Joan designs a necklace using Perspex quadrilaterals.

The dimensions of each shape used are shown on the next page.

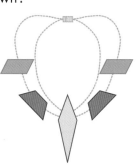

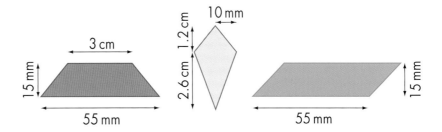

a Calculate the area of each of the shapes shown.

b Calculate the total area of each colour of Perspex needed in cm².

4 A side view of a wooden garden shed is shown.

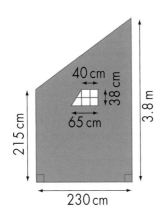

a Calculate the total area of the side view of the shed in square metres.

b What is the area of the window?

c What area of the side of the shed is wooden?

5 In art, Dawn is asked to draw four different quadrilaterals which have an area of 35 cm². Look at her four designs and decide which ones are correct.

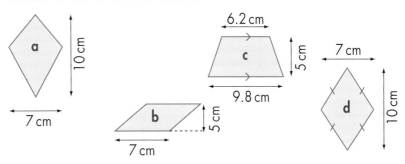

Exercise 11e

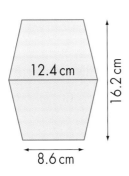

1 Two isosceles trapezia are placed edge to edge as shown in blue.

a Name the blue shape shown.

b Calculate the total area of the blue shape.

2 The diagram shows part of a border tile pattern on a bathroom wall.

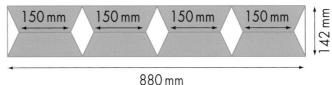

a What is the depth of one tile?

b Find the area of one trapezium.

c Find the ratio of the tile area which is white to green.

3 Martha is sewing a pattern to put on a quilt, using different shapes. The white circle has a diameter of 3 cm and the blue circle has a radius of 3 cm.

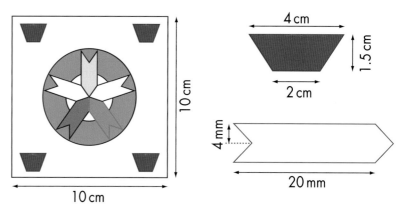

Give all answers in square centimetres.

a Calculate the area of blue material needed for the circle.

b How much pink material is needed?

c Calculate the total area of the five arrowheads.

d What fraction of the square pattern is white?

4 Bill is cutting out a card template for a boat.

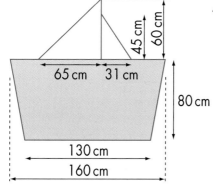

a Calculate the area of card he will need to the nearest square centimetre.

b He intends to cover the sails with white material. How much material will he need to buy? Give the answer to the nearest square centimetre.

c How many cm² are there in 1 m²?

d Convert the area of material needed into m².

e The material costs £4.99 per m². How much will the material cost to cover the sails?

5 A rectangular rug measures 1.8 m long by 120 cm wide.

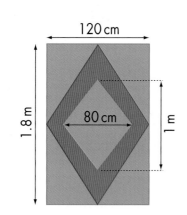

a Calculate the area of the rug. Give the answer in square metres.

b What area of the rug is red? Give the answer in square metres.

Consolidation Exercise

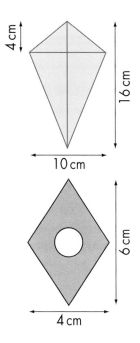

1 A rhombus has a perimeter of 80 cm.

   a What is the length of each side of the rhombus?

   The length of the shorter diagonal is 24 cm.

   b What is the area of the rhombus, if the other diagonal is 32 cm long?

2 Fred makes a kite frame out of sticks.

   a He covers the wooden frame with material. How much material will he need?

   b He cuts the kite out of a rectangular sheet measuring 14 cm by 18 cm. How much of the rectangle is wasted?

3 A metal brooch is made by cutting a circle, radius 1.5 cm, out of the middle of a rhombus. What area of metal is required to make the brooch?

4 The diagram shows markings on a road.

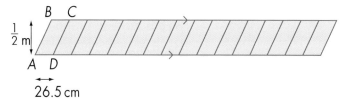

   a Calculate the area of *ABCD* in square centimetres.

   b Find the total area of road enclosed in the chevrons in m².

5 Disabled parking spaces are marked out in the diagram.

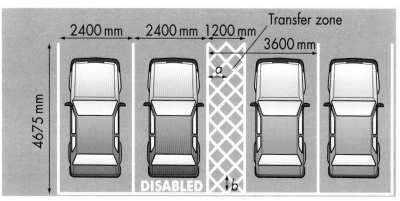

   a Calculate the total length of white line around the disabled car space. Give the answer in metres.

   b What is the area of an ordinary parking space in square metres? Give the answer correct to one decimal place.

   c Calculate the distance marked *a*.

   d Calculate the distance marked *b*.

   e What area is enclosed within a rhombus in the transfer zone in mm²? Convert the answer to square metres.

 **Fractions and decimals**

In this chapter, I am learning to:

- add and subtract fractions and mixed numbers
- calculate fractions of whole number quantities and round answers
- multiply fractions and decimals between 0 and 1.

Discussion 12.1

Joey and Judy are sharing a pack of peanuts. Joey eats $\frac{3}{8}$ of the pack while Judy eats $\frac{2}{5}$ of the pack. Joey says he has eaten $\frac{1}{3}$ more of the pack than Judy. How has Joey found this fraction? Do you agree with him? Explain your answer with reasons. Who has eaten the most nuts and by how much? What fraction of the pack remains?

Describe how to calculate $\frac{3}{8} - \frac{3}{4} + \frac{9}{16}$.

Exercise 12a

Simplify your answers where possible.

1 Calculate

a $\frac{1}{4} + \frac{3}{8}$ b $\frac{1}{12} + \frac{3}{4}$ c $\frac{1}{2} + \frac{5}{16}$

d $\frac{2}{3} + \frac{1}{4}$ e $\frac{1}{4} + \frac{1}{3} + \frac{1}{5}$ f $\frac{7}{30} + \frac{2}{15} + \frac{1}{3} + \frac{3}{10}$

2 Calculate

a $\frac{9}{10} - \frac{3}{5}$ b $\frac{5}{12} - \frac{1}{3}$ c $\frac{7}{8} - \frac{2}{3}$

d $\frac{4}{5} - \frac{3}{4}$ e $\frac{13}{20} - \frac{3}{8}$ f $1 - \frac{7}{16}$

3 Calculate

a $\frac{2}{3} + \frac{1}{12} - \frac{3}{8}$ b $\frac{3}{4} - \frac{2}{5} + \frac{1}{10}$ c $\frac{2}{9} - \frac{1}{2} + \frac{11}{18}$

d $\frac{1}{4} - \frac{1}{3} + \frac{1}{2} - \frac{1}{6}$

4 Sophie carried out a survey of teachers' cars. She found that $\frac{1}{4}$ of the cars were German, $\frac{1}{3}$ French and $\frac{1}{6}$ Spanish. Sophie listed the remaining cars as 'Other'. What fraction of cars were 'Other'?

5 Ryan surveys how his class travel to school. $\frac{1}{12}$ of his class walk, $\frac{3}{8}$ travel by bus, $\frac{1}{4}$ get a lift, $\frac{1}{24}$ cycle and the rest travel by taxi. What fraction travel by taxi?

6 Ronan supports his local football team. Last season the club's strikers scored $\frac{3}{5}$ of the team's goals, midfielders scored $\frac{3}{10}$ of the goals and defenders scored $\frac{1}{25}$ of the goals.

   a What fraction of the club's goals was scored by defenders, midfielders or strikers?

   b Is this the answer you expected? Try to explain how this result could be correct.

7 Gemma's hockey team won $\frac{1}{3}$ of their games last year, drew $\frac{2}{7}$ and lost the rest.

   a What fraction of games did the team lose?

   b List the results by outcome in ascending order.

8 Hannah has a 1 litre bottle of water. If she drinks $\frac{1}{2}$ a litre at break and $\frac{1}{3}$ of a litre at lunch, can she drink $\frac{1}{4}$ of a litre with her dinner? Explain your answer.

9 The visitors to Belfast Zoo one Saturday over Easter were recorded. $\frac{2}{7}$ of the visitors were boys and $\frac{1}{3}$ were girls.

   a What fraction of the total visitors were children?

   b What fraction were adults?

   c If there was an equal amount of men and women, what fraction of the visitors were women?

10 Use a calculator to check your answers to questions in this exercise.

Activity 12.1

Activity Sheet 12.1

Activity 12.2

Activity Sheet 12.2

Discussion 12.2

Rufus walks $1\frac{1}{4}$ miles to his friend Martha's house. Together they walk another $\frac{3}{8}$ of a mile to Loudon's house. How could you find the total distance Rufus has walked? What is different about this sum? What is $1\frac{1}{4}$ as an improper fraction? Rewrite the calculation using the improper fraction and find how far Rufus walked. Give your answer as both a mixed number and an improper fraction. How can $1\frac{1}{4}$ and $\frac{3}{8}$ be added without changing $1\frac{1}{4}$ to an improper fraction?

Claire wants to work out $3\frac{1}{3} - 2\frac{1}{2}$. She starts off by subtracting the whole number parts to get $3 - 2 = 1$. She then tries to work out $\frac{1}{3}$ take away $\frac{1}{2}$ and quickly becomes confused. What is the problem with her method? Can you think of an alternative method to help Claire solve her problem? Which method do you prefer?

Example 12.1

Work out $2\frac{1}{2} + 2\frac{2}{3} + 5\frac{1}{4}$ by

a first adding the whole numbers then the fractional parts

b changing all the mixed numbers to improper fractions first, then adding.

a $2\frac{1}{2} + 2\frac{2}{3} + 5\frac{1}{4} = 2 + 2 + 5 + \frac{1}{2} + \frac{2}{3} + \frac{1}{4} = 9 + \frac{6}{12} + \frac{8}{12} + \frac{3}{12}$

$= 9 + \frac{17}{12} = 9 + 1\frac{5}{12} = 10\frac{5}{12}$

b $2\frac{1}{2} + 2\frac{2}{3} + 5\frac{1}{4} = \frac{5}{2} + \frac{8}{3} + \frac{21}{4} = \frac{30}{12} + \frac{32}{12} + \frac{63}{12} = \frac{125}{12} = 10\frac{5}{12}$

Exercise 12b

Simplify your answers where possible.

1 Calculate

  a $\frac{7}{4} + \frac{5}{6}$ **b** $\frac{5}{3} + \frac{9}{4}$ **c** $\frac{3}{2} + \frac{4}{3} + \frac{5}{4}$

  d $\frac{8}{5} - \frac{1}{2}$ **e** $\frac{7}{4} - \frac{4}{3}$ **f** $\frac{9}{2} - \frac{13}{6}$

2 Calculate

  a $\frac{11}{3} - \frac{9}{4} - \frac{7}{6}$ **b** $\frac{3}{4} + \frac{7}{8} - \frac{21}{16}$ **c** $1\frac{3}{10} + \frac{3}{5}$

  d $3\frac{5}{8} + 2\frac{1}{2}$ **e** $1\frac{1}{3} + 2\frac{3}{8} + \frac{5}{12}$

3 Calculate

  a $3 - 1\frac{7}{8}$ **b** $8\frac{1}{6} - 5\frac{1}{4}$ **c** $7\frac{9}{16} - \frac{3}{8}$

  d $5\frac{4}{9} - 3\frac{17}{18}$ **e** $8\frac{3}{4} - 1\frac{5}{6} + 2\frac{1}{3}$ **f** $3\frac{3}{5} - 4\frac{7}{10} + 2\frac{1}{8}$

4 Pete watched $1\frac{1}{2}$ hours TV on Monday, $\frac{3}{4}$ hour on Tuesday and $2\frac{1}{4}$ hours on Wednesday. What was Pete's total viewing time over the three days?

5 Julie cuts $3\frac{3}{8}$ m from a 5 m roll of material. What length is left on the roll?

6 Sally and Simon watch TV. Sally watches a film lasting $1\frac{2}{3}$ hours. Her brother Simon watches a football match lasting $1\frac{3}{4}$ hours. Who has spent more time watching TV and by what fraction of an hour?

7 Find the perimeters of the shapes.

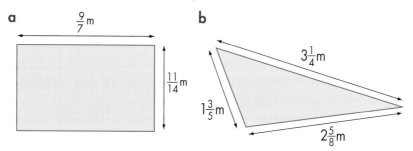

a $\frac{9}{7}$ m $\frac{11}{14}$ m

b $3\frac{1}{4}$ m $1\frac{3}{5}$ m $2\frac{5}{8}$ m

8 A lorry and its load weigh $12\frac{7}{8}$ tonnes. If the load weighs $5\frac{5}{12}$ tonnes, how heavy is the lorry?

9 Is it possible to cut off two pieces of wood, one $25\frac{5}{12}$ cm long, the other $31\frac{2}{3}$ cm from a piece that is 57 cm long? Explain your answer.

10 Use a calculator to check your answers to this exercise.

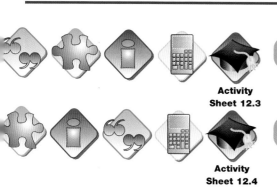

Activity 12.3

Activity Sheet 12.3

Activity 12.4

Activity Sheet 12.4

Discussion 12.3

Sammy's **gross pay** is £21 567.47 per annum. What is gross pay? If Sammy's total deductions come to $\frac{1}{4}$ of his gross pay what fraction of his pay is left? This amount is his **net pay**. How could you find the amount of Sammy's net pay without using a calculator? Estimate Sammy's net pay. If Sammy wants to find his net pay accurate to the nearest penny to how many decimal places should he work? Example 12.2 shows how to find his net pay accurate to the nearest penny.

Example 12.2

Find $\frac{1}{4}$ of Sammy's gross pay by dividing by 4. Note that a zero is added and the answer is worked out to three decimal places.

$$4 \,\big|\, £2\overset{2}{1}5\overset{1}{6}7.\overset{3}{4}\overset{3}{7}\overset{2}{0}$$
$$5391.867$$

So $\frac{1}{4}$ of £21 567.47 is £5391.87 to the nearest penny.

Sammy's net pay is then found either by subtracting this amount from his gross pay or by multiplying by 3 to give $\frac{3}{4}$ of his gross pay, as shown.

$$\begin{array}{r} £\;21567.47 \\ -\;£\;\;\;5391.87 \\ \hline £\;16175.60 \end{array} \qquad \begin{array}{r} £\;5391.87 \\ \times\;\;\;\;\;3 \\ \hline £16175.61 \end{array}$$

Which of these answers is more accurate and why?

The answer by subtraction is slightly more accurate as the **rounding error**, which was introduced when rounding one quarter of Sammy's gross pay to two decimal places, has not been allowed to increase further by multiplying it by three.

Exercise 12c

1 Mike earns £42 372 gross per annum.

   a He pays $\frac{1}{12}$ of his gross pay into a company pension fund. How much is this?

   b Income tax and national insurance are deducted at a rate of $\frac{4}{11}$ from Mike's gross pay. What do these deductions total?

   c After deductions, what is Mike's net pay?

2 Calculate the answers to the degree of accuracy stated in brackets.

   a $\frac{2}{3}$ of 17 cm (one decimal place)

   b $\frac{5}{7}$ of 82 litres (three decimal places)

   c $\frac{11}{13}$ of 20 m (two decimal places)

   d $\frac{6}{5}$ of 213 kg (two significant figures)

   e $2\frac{3}{8}$ of 133 ml (four significant figures)

   f $\frac{15}{7}$ of 875 g (three significant figures)

3 Collette buys a new car costing £11 995. By the time it needs its first service, its value has depreciated by $\frac{2}{7}$. What is it worth when it has its first service? Give your answer to a sensible degree of accuracy.

4 Jake weighs 43 kg. His brother Corey is $\frac{4}{3}$ his weight. What weight, in kilograms, is Corey, accurate to three significant figures?

5 Avril, Paul, Clifford and Ralph share a £7 127 football pools win.

    a If Avril gets $\frac{1}{3}$ of the winnings, Paul $\frac{1}{4}$, Clifford $\frac{1}{5}$ and Ralph the rest of the win, what fraction of the winnings does Ralph receive?

    b How much is each person's share?

6 Find $\frac{4}{7}$ of 13 accurate to **a** one **b** two **c** three **d** four significant figures.

7 Cecil buys the following goods exclusive of VAT.

    a The VAT rate of 17.5% is equivalent to $\frac{7}{40}$ of the price. Find the VAT payable on each item.

    b Find the total price paid for the items inclusive of VAT at 17.5%.

    c Find $\frac{47}{40}$ of £398. What do you notice? Explain your answer.

8 Rafael earns £11 an hour. His overtime rate is paid at time and three quarters. How much does he earn for one hour's overtime?

9 A survey of 2000 adults in Northern Ireland reported that $\frac{5}{7}$ of the population regularly send e-mails.

    a How many adults surveyed regularly send e-mails?

    b Is it possible for exactly $\frac{5}{7}$ of the population to send e-mails?

    Give a reason for your answer. Why do you think $\frac{5}{7}$ was chosen as the fraction in the report?

10 Use a calculator to check your answers for this exercise.

Activity 12.5

Activity Sheet 12.5

Discussion 12.4

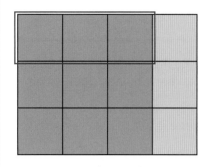

Which is the smaller fraction, $\frac{1}{3}$ or $\frac{3}{4}$? Is $\frac{1}{3}$ of $\frac{3}{4}$ bigger or smaller than 1?

Explain why $\frac{1}{3}$ of $\frac{3}{4}$ must be less than both $\frac{3}{4}$ and $\frac{1}{3}$. Use the diagram to help you find the value of $\frac{1}{3}$ of $\frac{3}{4}$.

In maths we sometimes replace the word 'of' by a multiplication sign. So $\frac{1}{3}$ of $\frac{3}{4}$ can be rewritten as $\frac{1}{3} \times \frac{3}{4}$ which equals $\frac{1}{4}$. Look at the pairs of fractions which have been multiplied.

$$\frac{1}{2} \times \frac{1}{4} = \frac{1}{8} \qquad \frac{2}{3} \times \frac{1}{3} = \frac{2}{9} \qquad \frac{3}{5} \times \frac{2}{7} = \frac{6}{35}$$

Try to find a relationship between the numerators in the given fractions and the numerators in the product.

Now find a relationship for the denominators.

What is $\frac{2}{3} \times \frac{4}{5}$ equal to? Is this answer smaller than both $\frac{2}{3}$ and $\frac{4}{5}$?

What is the product of any 2 fractions, $\frac{a}{b} \times \frac{c}{d}$?

Example 12.3

Find the product of $\frac{3}{4}$ and $\frac{2}{5}$ and give your answer in its lowest terms.

Solution 1: $\frac{3}{4} \times \frac{2}{5} = \frac{6}{20} = \frac{3}{10}$ (cancelling at the end)

or

Solution 2: $_2\frac{3}{4} \times \frac{\cancel{2}^{1}}{5} = \frac{3}{10}$ (cancelling common factors first)

Remember that fractions will cancel when the numerator and the denominator have factors in common.

Exercise 12d

1 Calculate

a $\frac{1}{5} \times \frac{1}{6}$ b $\frac{2}{3} \times \frac{1}{7}$ c $\frac{4}{5} \times \frac{4}{5}$ d $\frac{3}{8} \times \frac{5}{7}$

e $\frac{9}{11} \times \frac{2}{5}$ f $\frac{3}{7} \times \frac{1}{2}$ g $\frac{7}{8} \times \frac{9}{10}$ h $\left(\frac{3}{10}\right)^2$

2 Calculate

a $\frac{7}{12} \times \frac{3}{14}$ b $\frac{2}{3} \times \frac{5}{8}$ c $\frac{4}{9} \times \frac{3}{11}$ d $\frac{3}{4} \times \frac{8}{21}$

e $\frac{4}{15} \times \frac{35}{64}$ f $\frac{2}{3}$ of $\frac{19}{14}$ g $\left(\frac{5}{6}\right)^2 \times \frac{24}{35}$

3 Did you use the same method for Question **1** as for Question **2**? If you changed method, explain how this was helpful.

4 Three-fifths of pupils in year 8 own a calculator. Two-thirds of these calculators are scientific. What fraction of pupils in the year group own scientific calculators?

5 Find the product of these fractions

   a $\frac{2}{3} \times \frac{3}{4} \times \frac{4}{5}$ **b** $\frac{5}{11} \times \frac{2}{35} \times \frac{4}{9}$ **c** $\frac{1}{2} \times \frac{7}{10} \times \left(\frac{2}{5}\right)^2$

   d $\frac{3}{13} \times \frac{12}{17} \times \frac{39}{51} \times \frac{34}{45}$

6 Check your answers to this exercise with a calculator.

Discussion 12.5

What is the product of $\frac{1}{10}$ and $\frac{3}{10}$? What is the product of 0.1 and 0.3? How could you find the product of 0.15 and 0.3? What is this product as a fraction? What is this as a decimal? If a and b are decimal values greater than 0 and smaller than 1, what can be said about their product?

Example 12.4

Find the product of 0.3 and 0.72.

Rewrite the decimals as fractions, then multiply:

$\frac{3}{10} \times \frac{72}{100} = \frac{216}{1000} = 0.216$

The product of 0.3 and 0.72 is 0.216 as a decimal or $\frac{27}{125}$ as fraction in its lowest terms.

Exercise 12e

1 Find the product of the following decimals by changing them into fractions first. Give your answer both as a fraction, in its lowest terms, and as a decimal.

   a 0.2×0.5 **b** 0.4×0.8 **c** 0.3×0.9

   d 0.12×0.1 **e** 0.35×0.6 **f** 0.08×0.9

   g 0.07×0.05 **h** 0.008×0.6 **i** 0.85×0.15

   j $0.5 \times 0.04 \times 0.003$

2 a Repeat Question 1, using a calculator and give your answers as decimals.

   b Do all of your answers agree with this statement?

     *If **a** and **b** are decimal numbers greater than 0 but less than 1, then the product of **a** and **b** must be less than both **a** and **b**.*

3 In this question do not use a calculator or change the decimals into fractions. You should be able to just write down the answer using your knowledge of decimals and place value.

a What is 8 times 5?

b What is 0.8 times 5?

c What is 0.8 times 0.5?

d What is 0.08 times 0.5?

e What is 0.08 times 0.05?

4 Find the value of x in each of the following:

a $0.7 \times x = 0.35$ **b** $0.1 \times x = 0.04$

c $x \times 0.7 = 0.28$ **d** $0.15 \times x = 0.045$

e $0.5 \times x \times 0.04 = 0.0006$

Consolidation Exercise

1 Look at these fractions: $\frac{7}{15}, \frac{49}{90}, \frac{11}{30}$

a arrange them in ascending order

b subtract the smallest fraction from the largest

c find the sum of the three fractions

d what fraction lies midway between the smallest and largest fractions?

2 A company director is entitled to $\frac{2}{15}$ of his firm's profits. What amount does the director receive if the firm makes a profit of £211 072?

3 Calculate

a $1\frac{2}{5} + \frac{3}{8}$ **b** $3\frac{5}{6} - 2\frac{3}{4}$ **c** $\frac{5}{4} - 1\frac{1}{6} + \frac{7}{12}$

4 Multiply these fractions.

a $\frac{1}{4} \times \frac{2}{7}$ **b** $\frac{2}{3} \times \frac{5}{8}$ **c** $\frac{7}{8} \times \frac{5}{9}$ **d** $\frac{4}{9} \times \frac{15}{16}$

e $\frac{4}{7} \times \frac{35}{63}$ **f** $\left(\frac{2}{9}\right)^2$ **g** $\frac{42}{55} \times \frac{15}{21}$ **h** $\frac{5}{7} \times \frac{14}{21}$

i $\frac{4}{5} \times \frac{55}{64}$ **j** $\frac{13}{15} \times \frac{33}{52}$ **k** $\frac{3}{8}$ of $\frac{12}{25}$

5 Jason earns £17 643 gross pay annually. If his deductions for income tax, national insurance and pension come to $\frac{3}{11}$ of his salary what is his net pay?

6 a Evaluate 0.032×0.4

b Evaluate $\frac{16}{1000} \times \frac{8}{10}$

c Comment on your answers.

13 Time, distance and speed

In this chapter, I am learning to

- carry out calculations involving time, distance and speed
- interpret and construct distance–time graphs
- carry out speed calculations using imperial and metric units of distance.

Discussion 13.1

In 2003 Paula Radcliffe set a World record for running the women's marathon in a time of 2:15:25. Can you explain what this time means?

In the same year a Chinese athlete took 2h 19 minutes and 39s to run the marathon. How much slower is 2 h 19 minutes and 39s than 2:15:25?

Exercise 13a

1   In a race, James's time was 39.56 seconds and Ben's time was 46.69 seconds. Who was faster and by how much?

2   The times for the school's yellow house relay team are shown.

Runner	1	2	3	4
Time (s)	22.5	23.28	21.5	20.19

   a   What was the team's total time?

   b   How many seconds difference was there between the fastest and the slowest times?

   c   The green house also competed in the relay race and their results are shown in the table.

Runner	1	2	3	4
Time (s)	19.43	24.37	17.5	25

   Compare the times for the two houses. Which house do you think had a stronger team?

3 The table shows the time taken to run a half marathon. Damien runs quickly, Howard runs it at a moderate pace and Hilary takes it easy.

Name	Damien	Howard	Hilary
Time taken	147 minutes	210 minutes	262.5 minutes

   a How much longer did it take Hilary than Damien?

   b How many seconds later than Howard did Hilary arrive at the finish line?

   c A half marathon is approximately 21 km. How many metres did each person run in 1 minute? Give your answer correct to the nearest metre.

4 In the 2008 Summer Olympics the women's 3000 m steeplechase race took place for the first time. The final results are given in the table.

Rank	Name	Nationality	Time
1	Gulnara Samitova-Galkina	Russia	8:58.81
2	Eunice Jepkorir	Kenya	9:07.41
3	Yekaterina Volkova	Russia	9:07.64
4	Tatyana Petrova	Russia	9:12.33
5	Cristina Casandra	Romania	9:16.85
6	Ruth Bisibori Nyangau	Kenya	9:17.35
7	Zemzem Ahmed	Ethiopia	9:17.85
8	Wioletta Frankiewicz	Poland	9:21.76
9	Jennifer Barringer	United States	9:22.26
10	Anna Willard	United States	9:25.63
11	Elena Romagnolo	Italy	9:30.04
12	Zulema Fuentes-Pila	Spain	9:35.16
13	Habiba Ghribi	Tunisia	9:36.43
14	Roisin McGettigan	Ireland	9:55.89

   a What is the time difference between the fastest and slowest runners?

   b Calculate the speed of each competitor in m/s.

5 Zola Budd twice broke the world record in the women's 5000 m. In 1984 she ran the race in a time of 15:01.83. The following year she surpassed her previous world record by clocking 14:49.47.

   a By how many seconds did she reduce her time?

   b Calculate her average speed over both races.

Discussion 13.2

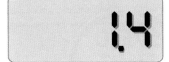

Thomas is using his calculator to do time calculations and gets an answer of 1.4 hours.

He says the answer is 1 hour 40 minutes. Is he correct? Give a reason for your answer.

A calculator display shows the answer to a time calculation as 1.75 hours. What is the answer in minutes? Give a reason for your answer.

James wants to change times given in minutes into hours. Can you help him to convert each of these to hours:

a 30 minutes   **b** 45 minutes   **c** 6 minutes

Explain how you got your answers.

If you gave your answers using fractions now write them as decimals.

What is 2 hours 15 minutes written as a decimal time? Explain your working.

When using a calculator to carry out time calculations remember that it uses the decimal system and base 10 while time calculations involving minutes and seconds are in base 60.

0.1 hour = $\frac{1}{10}$ of an hour = $\frac{1}{10}$ of 60 minutes = 6 minutes

Exercise 13b

SUS13b

Copy and complete the following table. Round the calculator answers correct to two decimal places, where necessary.

	Time	Time in decimal form
1	50 minutes	h
2	42 minutes	h
3	2h 20 minutes	h
4	$2\frac{2}{3}$ h	h
5	3h 40 minutes	h
6	5h 25 minutes	h
7	95 minutes	h
8	minutes	2.75h
9	h minutes	10.2h
10	h minutes	3.45h
11	minutes	0.9h
12	minutes	1.666666667h

1 mile is approximately 1.6 km

Discussion 13.3

Look at the two road signs.

Do they both indicate the same speed limit? Explain your answer.

If you are told that the sign on the left is in Belfast and the sign on the right is in Dublin, would you still give the same answer to the question?

What is actually meant by a speed of 60 mph?

What is meant by a speed of 60 km/h?

Using the equivalence between miles and kilometres, which car would be travelling faster: a car going at a speed of 60 mph or a car travelling at a speed of 60 km/h? Explain your answer. Suggest why the speed limits in different units may cause problems for motorists.

Speed measures the **distance** which can be travelled over a certain period of time. The units of speed denote the time period. For example, **mph** indicates the number of miles covered in 1 hour. Similarly **m/s** indicates the number of metres travelled in 1 second.

Discussion 13.4

Suggest some other units of speed.

If a snail travels a distance of 20 millimetres over a period of 10 seconds, what unit would you use to calculate its speed?

What unit of speed would you use to state how fast you can walk?

What could the abbreviated unit m/min represent?

Do you know what unit of measure is used to measure the speed of boats?

Activity
Sheet 13.1

Activity 13.1

Activity
Sheet 13.2

Activity 13.2

Discussion 13.5

If a car travels 145 miles in 3 hours, how far does the car travel in 1 hour? What is the speed of the car?

In a real-life situation does this mean that the car is travelling at this speed for the entire journey? Explain your answer.

Average speed can be calculated by using the formula

$$S = \frac{D}{T}$$

where **D** is the total distance travelled in the complete journey

and **T** is the time taken to complete the journey.

Similarly the time and distance can be calculated by rearranging this formula.

Time = **D**istance ÷ **S**peed   **D**istance = **S**peed × **T**ime

Example 13.1

Gareth takes 25 seconds to run a distance of 120 metres. Find his speed.

$$S = \frac{D}{T}$$

$$S = 120 \text{ m} \div 25 \text{s}$$

$$S = 4.8 \text{ m/s}$$

Example 13.2

Freda travels 44 miles to work and the journey takes 45 minutes. Calculate her speed in miles per hour.

$$S = \frac{D}{T}$$

as the answer is required in miles per hour , the time *T* needs to be in *hours*

45 minutes = (45 ÷ 60)h = $\frac{3}{4}$ h = 0.75 h

$$S = 44 \div 0.75$$

$$S = 58.\dot{6} \text{ mph} = 58.7 \text{ mph (to 1 d.p.)}$$

Example 13.3

Gavin lives 66 miles from Belfast. If he travels at an average speed of 55mph, how many minutes will the journey from his home to Belfast take?

$$T = \frac{D}{S}$$

$$T = \frac{66 \text{ miles}}{55 \text{ miles per hour}} = 1.2\,h = 1.2 \times 60 \text{ minutes} = 72 \text{ minutes}$$

Exercise 13c

Runner	Time
Geordie	15s
Frankie	10.5s
Harry	10.39s
Finbar	10.18s
Wallie	9.98s

1 An aeroplane flies 3400 km in 4 hours at a constant speed.

   a How far does the plane fly in 1 hour?

   b How far will the plane fly in $3\frac{1}{2}$ hours at the same speed?

2 The table shows the results of a 100 m race. Calculate the average speed of each runner in m/s, correct to two decimal places.

3 A car completes a journey of 240 km in $2\frac{1}{2}$ hours. What was the average speed of the car?

4 It is said that males over 60 years old walk at an average speed of 1.1 m/s and females over 60 walk at an average speed of 1.15 m/s. John wants to calculate how much further a female over 60 will have walked than a male of the same age in 20 minutes.

   a How many seconds are in 20 minutes?

   b How much further will the female have walked than a male of the same age in 20 minutes?

5 Joel is travelling from Belfast International Airport to Lisburn, a distance of 22 km. If he travels at a steady speed of 55 km/h, how many minutes will the journey take?

6 Henry drives for 40 minutes at an average speed of 66 mph. How far has he travelled?

7 Jane travels 22 miles to work and takes 18 minutes to arrive at her destination. John takes 30 minutes to travel 35 miles to work.

   a Calculate Jane's speed in miles per hour, to one decimal place.

   b Calculate John's speed in miles per hour.

   c If the speed limit is 60mph, who is exceeding the speed limit?

8 The Wright brothers flew a distance of 38 958 metres in 38 minutes and 13 seconds.

   a How many seconds is 38 minutes and 13 seconds?

   b What was this speed in m/s?

9 The fastest speed of a tennis ball served was by Andy Roddick 155mph or 294 km/h.

  a How many miles could the ball travel in 1 hour, if we ignore other external factors?

  b What external factors might affect the speed of the ball?

  c Work out the number of metres the ball will travel in 1 second, if the speed remains constant.

Activity
Sheet 13.3

Activity 13.3

Distance–time graphs

A journey can be shown by using a travel graph or a **distance–time graph**. The time is always shown on the horizontal scale and the distance on the vertical scale.

Discussion 13.6

Keera lives 10 kilometres from school. She gets a bus to school each morning and returns home from school by bus. The graph shows Keera's journey to and from school.

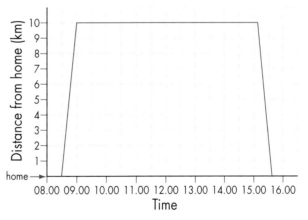

Before reading a graph it is important to understand the horizontal and vertical scales. On the horizontal scale what does the width of one square represent? What distance does the height of one square represent on the vertical scale?

What does the horizontal line on the graph represent?

Exercise 13d

In each of the following questions study the scales carefully before answering the questions.

1   Laura works in a shop which is 30 km from her home. The travel graph shows her journey to and from work each day. Use the graph to answer the following questions.

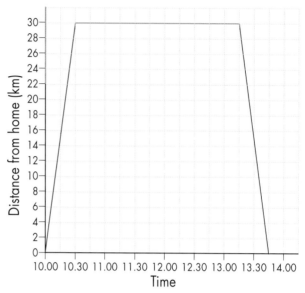

a   What time does Laura leave home in the morning?

b   How long does she take to travel to work?

c   How many hours does Laura work?

d   At what time does she arrive home?

2   The graph shows Larry's distance from home on a cycle trip with his friends.

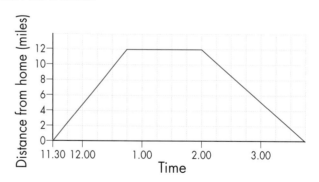

a   What length of time does the width of one square on the horizontal scale represent?

b   What does the height of one square on the vertical scale represent?

c   How far away from home did he travel?

d   Describe what was happening between a quarter to one and two o'clock.

e   How long was Larry away from home altogether?

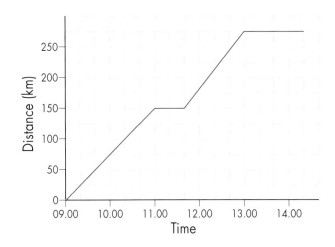

3 The travel graph shows a salesman's journey.

   a How long did the salesman travel before he stopped for his first break?

   b For how long did he stop?

   c Describe the salesman's journey.

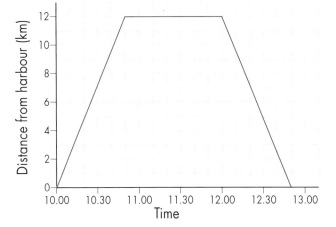

4 When Eve is on holiday in France, she goes on a ferry trip from the harbour to a small island.

   a How long did the ferry journey from the harbour to the island take?

   b How many kilometres is the island away from the harbour?

   c How long did Eve spend on the island before returning back to the harbour?

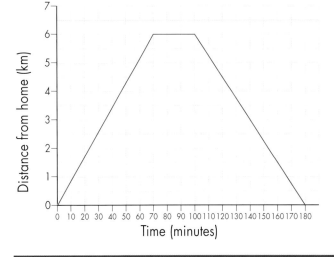

5 Barney goes for a long walk from home to the local beauty spot and back. The graph shows his journey. Describe his journey in detail.

Activity Sheet 13.4

Activity 13.4

When you look at the slope of the line on a distance–time graph you will notice a difference in the steepness. In maths the slope of the line is known as the **gradient**. The **gradient** of the line shows the speed.

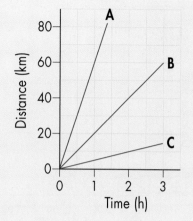

The steepest line **A** shows a speed of 60 km/h while the next steepest line **B** has a speed of 20 km/h. Line **C** has the least slope and indicates a speed of 5 km/h.

The **steeper** the **gradient,** the **faster** the speed.

Example 13.4

Mr and Mrs Commuter travel from their home in Antrim to work in Belfast. Mrs Commuter travels by bus while Mr Commuter travels by car. The journey to work is 20 miles.

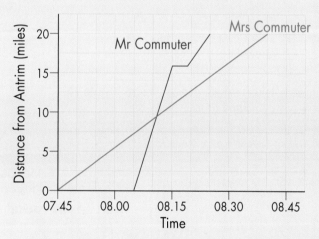

a Use the graph to calculate the average speed of each journey to work.

b Mr Commuter is caught in rush hour traffic while the bus is not. Can you give a reason for this?

c Does Mr Commuter travel faster before or after he has been stopped?

a Mr Commuter's average speed = total distance ÷ total time
= 20 ÷ 0.6 = 33⅓ mph

Mrs Commuter's average speed = total distance ÷ total time = 20 ÷ 0.9 = 22.2 mph

b Bus can travel along the bus lane

c The gradient of the line is steeper before he stops than after so he travelled faster before he stopped (average speed of 64 mph). His average speed after the stop was 48 mph.

Discussion 13.7

In a bid to make commuting more eco-friendly, the Government has suggested how fuel emissions can be reduced. Suggest ways Mr and Mrs Commuter could help protect the environment. How do you think road users in Northern Ireland could reduce emissions? What problems might this have for some travellers?

Exercise 13e

1   The graph shows the progress of two competitors in a 100 m race.

  a By looking at the slope of the graphs, can you say which runner is faster?

  b Work out the average speed of both runners. Round your answer to two decimal places where necessary.

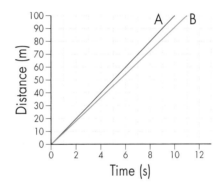

2   The graph shows the journey of an airport bus travelling to Dublin.

  a Describe the journey.

  b Calculate the speed of the bus during the first stage of the journey.

  c Calculate the speed of the bus during the second stage of the journey.

  d Calculate the overall average speed for the entire journey.

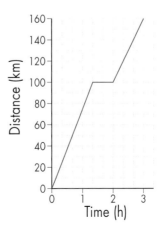

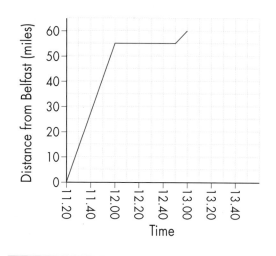

3   Hilary is travelling by direct bus from Belfast to Coleraine and then has to wait for a train to travel to Portrush.

The graph shows her journey. Use the graph to answer the questions.

a   How many miles is it from Belfast to Coleraine?

b   Calculate the speed of the bus.

c   How long does Hilary have to wait in Coleraine for the train to Portrush?

d   At what speed was the train travelling?

Consolidation Exercise

1   How do you convert mph to km/h?

2   Simon says that a speed of 1 m/s is the same as a speed of 4 km/h. Is he correct? Show calculations to support your answer.

3   Frances travels for 25 minutes at a speed of 90 km/h. How far has she travelled?

4   Joanne travels a distance of 120 miles at a speed of 55 mph. How long does the journey take, assuming she travels at a steady speed?

5   Harold leaves home at 9.15 a.m. and drives 100 km to attend a meeting in Newtownards.

a   If he travels at a steady speed of 50 km/h, how long does the journey take?

b   His meeting lasts for $1\frac{3}{4}$ hours. At what time is the meeting over?

c   If he drives home at a steady speed of 80 km/h, at what time will he arrive home?

d   Draw a distance–time graph to show this journey. Use a vertical scale of 1 cm to 10 km and a horizontal scale of 1 cm to 1 hour.

6   The speed of the sound of thunder is approximately 760 mph.

a   Approximately how many kilometres per hour is 760 mph?

b   If the noise of thunder takes 8 seconds to reach the listener, approximately how far away is it in metres?

Task 3: A walk in the mountains

Ryan and Lucy are planning to walk a section of the Ulster Way in the Mourne Mountains.

They trace the route they are going to walk from a 1 : 25 000 map. Ask your teacher for a copy of this map.

Ryan and Lucy like to plan ahead so they have divided their walk into several legs and are drawing up a table showing how long each leg will take and the bearing they need to walk on from one leg to the next. Although they will be walking on a path for some of the way, they need to know the bearing in case of bad weather.

Assume a speed of 4 km per hour on the flat or going down hill.

For uphill legs, add 1 minute for each 10 m increase in height.

Your task is to:

● complete the bearing, distance and time columns in the table

● work out the total distance Ryan and Lucy will walk

● work out how long the walk will take them – see the important information below

● draw up a plan for the day's walking – include the starting time and don't forget to allow times for rests and to stop for snacks and lunch.

Important information for calculating times

Leg	From	Height	To	Height	Bearing	Distance (km)	Time (mins)
1	Ott Car Park	390 m	Road/path junction	380 m			
2	Road/path junction	380 m	Pigeon Rock summit	540 m			
3	Pigeon Rock Summit	540 m	Wall Corner	500 m			
4	Wall Corner	500 m	Path meets river	400 m			
5	Path meets river	400 m	Slieve Moughanmore summit	550 m			
6	Slieve Moughanmore summit	550 m	Windy Gap	400 m			
7	Windy Gap	400 m	Sandback Road Car Park	170 m			

14 Volume

In this chapter, I am learning to:

- calculate the volume of prisms and cylinders
- calculate volume using mixed units
- apply volume formulae to find the volume of composite shapes
- understand density and calculate the density of objects.

Discussion 14 .1

Rod and Gwen's teacher has asked them to calculate the volume of the storage box shown. Look at Rod and Gwen's methods to calculate the volume. Whose **method** is correct?

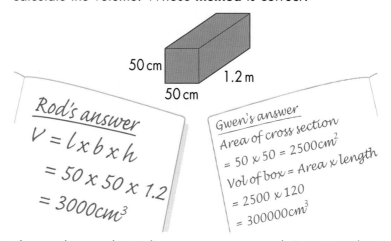

50 cm

50 cm

1.2 m

Rod's answer
$V = l \times b \times h$
$= 50 \times 50 \times 1.2$
$= 3000 cm^3$

Gwen's answer
Area of cross section
$= 50 \times 50 = 2500 cm^2$
Vol of box = Area × length
$= 2500 \times 120$
$= 300000 cm^3$

The teacher marks Rod's answer wrong and Gwen's right. Can you find the mistake?

Volume of cuboid = lbh

where l = length, b = breadth and h = height

The formula to find the area of the cross section of a cuboid is $A = lb$ so the formula to find the volume of a cuboid can be written as $V = Ah$.

Exercise 14a

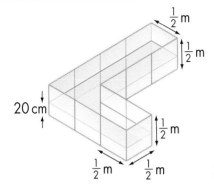

1 A playgroup has a water activity area for children. The play area is made from open cubes which have sides of length $\frac{1}{2}$ metre. The cubes are arranged in an L-shape as shown.

a Find the total volume of the cubes in cubic metres.

b For safety reasons, the cubes are filled with water to a depth of 20 cm. Find the volume of water needed for one cube.

c How many litres of water are needed to fill all the cubes to a depth of 20 cm? Remember 1 litre = 1000 cm³.

2 Harry is making a wooden mould to make two concrete steps for his back garden.

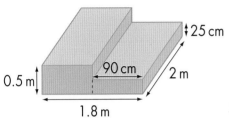

a Calculate how many square metres of wood he will need to make the mould, assuming that he is leaving the top open to pour in the concrete and the mould does not need a base.

b Calculate the volume of cement needed to make the steps.

3 Here is a desk.

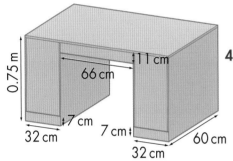

a Find the volume of the knee space.

b What is the total external volume of the cupboard space?

4 A storage box, in the shape of a closed cube, has a volume of 3375 cubic centimetres. The manufacturers wish to change the shape of the container to a cuboid while keeping the volume constant.

a If the base of the cuboid is 0.25 m long and 15 cm wide, what is the height of the cuboid?

b Suggest another possible set of dimensions for a cuboid which will have a volume of 3375 cubic centimetres.

c How much material is needed to make the original cube?

d What area of material would be needed to make the cuboid in a?

e Is your own suggestion more economical to make? Show working to support your answer.

5 Packaging for a set of four tumblers is shown in the diagram.

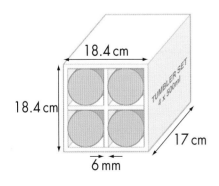

a Find the overall volume of the box, using the external dimensions.

b The box is made from cardboard that is 6 mm thick. Calculate the internal volume of the box.

c The interior of the box is subdivided into four sections to separate the tumblers. The width of the packaging is 6 mm. Find the volume of each individual section allocated to each tumbler in cm³.

d The tumblers are filled with paper to avoid breakages. Each tumbler holds 500 ml. What volume of each section is empty, if the thickness of the tumbler is ignored?

6 The coffee packet has a volume of 1038.8 cm³. Find the length of each side of the square base.

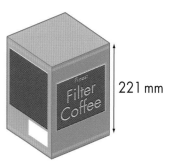

221 mm

Example 14.1

In everyday life not all three- dimensional shapes come in the form of cubes or cuboids.

The cross sectional area of the front of this garden shed consists of a **rectangle** and a **triangle**.

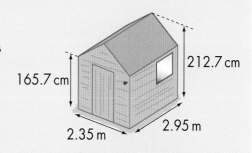

165.7 cm   212.7 cm

2.35 m   2.95 m

Area of rectangle = $l \times b$ = 2.35 × 1.657 = 3.89395 m²

To find the area of the triangle it is necessary to find its height first.

Height of triangle = 2.127 − 1.657 = 0.47 m

Area of triangle = $\frac{1}{2} \times b \times h$ = $\frac{1}{2}$ × 2.35 × 0.47 = 0.55225 m²

Total area of front of shed = 3.89395 + 0.55225 = 4.4462 m²

To find the volume of the shed use the formula $V = Ah$

Volume of shed = $A \times h$ = 4.4462 × 2.95 = 13.12 m³ (2 d.p.)

Discussion 14.2

Example 14.1 shows one possible method that can be used to find the volume of a shed. Discuss any other possible methods that could be used.

Exercise 14b

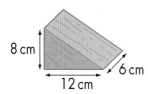

8 cm   6 cm   12 cm

1 A door wedge is made from wood.

a What is the mathematical name of this shape?

b What volume of wood is needed to make two of these wedges?

c If both wedges are cut from a single block of wood, draw two sketches to show two different blocks that they could be cut from.

2 The table shows the dimensions of other models of shed which are similar to the model in Example 14.1. For each shed calculate its volume to the nearest cubic metre.

Model	Width	Depth	Eaves height	Ridge height
A	195 cm	2.5 m	1.25 m	2.16 m
B	1.45 m	205 cm	1.657 m	1.917 m
C	205 cm	235 cm	165.7 cm	198.7 cm

3 Find the volume contained in the block of cheese of depth 2 cm.

4 a Taking the cross section of the wheelie bin to be a trapezium, calculate the approximate volume of the wheelie bin in cubic centimetres.

b Find the capacity of the bin in litres.

5 The column of basalt has a volume of 14 610 cm³ and is 1.5 m high. What is the area of the hexagonal face?

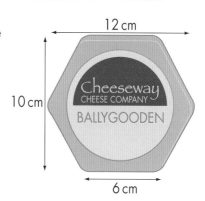

12 cm
10 cm
6 cm
Cheeseway
CHEESE COMPANY
BALLYGOODEN

1.5 m

60 cm
60 cm
1 m
40 cm
40 cm

Discussion 14.3

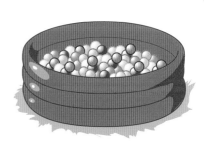

How can I estimate the volume of the balls inside the pool?

Discuss your ideas with other pupils in the class. What is the best method to use?

Example 14.2

Find the volume of the pool.

To find an accurate volume of the pool we can use the formula for the volume of a cylinder using **volume of cylinder = area of base × height**.

The base area is a circle $= \pi r^2$ so the **volume of cylinder** $= \pi r^2 \times h = \pi r^2 h$

Volume of pool $= \pi \times 50^2 \times 20 \text{ cm}^3$

Volume of pool $= 157\,079.6327\ldots \text{ cm}^3$

Since 1 cm^3 is equivalent to 1 ml, the volume of the pool is $157\,000 \text{ ml}$ or 157 litres correct to 3 significant figures.

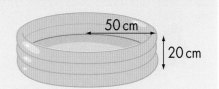

Volume of a cylinder $= \pi r^2 h$

where **r** is the radius and **h** is the height

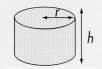

Exercise 14c

1 Find the volumes of the cylinders, showing your working clearly. Give the answer in the units indicated in brackets and round to the nearest whole unit.

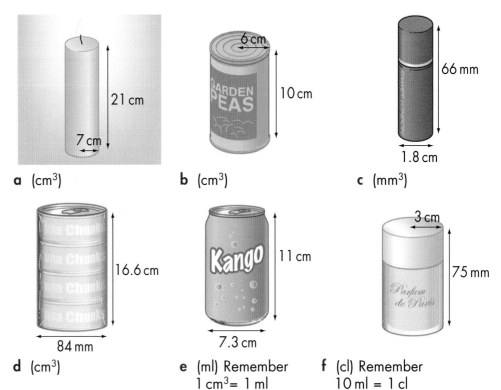

a (cm³)   b (cm³)   c (mm³)

d (cm³)   e (ml) Remember   f (cl) Remember
                     1 cm³= 1 ml   10 ml = 1 cl

154

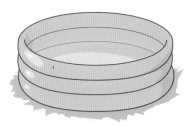

2 The paddling pool has an internal diameter of 1.5 m and a height of 55 cm.

   a Find the volume of the paddling pool in cm³.

   b Find the capacity of the paddling pool in litres. Give the answer correct to two significant figures.

3

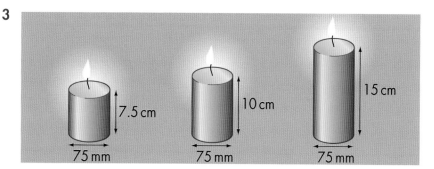

Find the total volume of wax needed to make the three pillar candles. Give the answer in cm³ to the nearest whole number.

4 The manufacturer claims that the play pool has a capacity of 500 litres. Show calculations to test this claim.

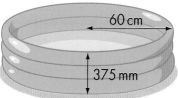

5 **a** Find the volume of the drum.

   b The drum is placed into a cuboid shaped box of length 20 cm, breadth 20 cm and height 12 cm. Find the volume of the cuboid.

   c What fraction of the space inside the box is empty?

6 A large tin of soup is poured into a saucepan.

   a Find the capacity of the soup tin in millilitres, correct to three significant figures.

   b What depth will the soup be when it is all poured from the can into the saucepan A? Give your answer to the nearest centimetre.

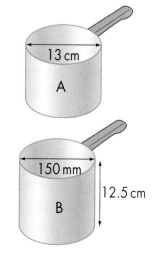

   c Sara opens another similar sized tin of soup and pours it into saucepan B. Will all of the soup fit into the saucepan?

     Show calculations to support your answer.

Exercise 14d

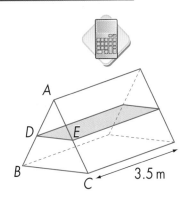

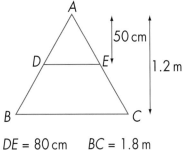

1 Drew is making a wooden frame for the roof of a playhouse. He draws a sketch to show the measurements of the end of the roof.

He places a support across the rafters 50 cm from the top of the roof.

DE = 80 cm   BC = 1.8 m

a If the playhouse is 3.5 m long, calculate the volume of the entire roof space in cubic metres.

b Drew plans to put up a ceiling along the line DE.

Calculate the volume of the roof space below the ceiling level.

2 George uses concrete pipes to drain his garden.

Each pipe has an internal diameter of 60 cm and the pipe width is 50 mm.

a George places a pipe in an upright position and closes off the bottom end of the pipe.

If the pipe fills up with rainwater what is the maximum volume that the pipe will hold?

b Calculate the volume of concrete required to make one pipe.

3 Three cylindrical tins of meat are packed into a box in the shape of a cuboid.

a Calculate the volume of packaging in cubic centimetres.

b What volume of the package is empty?

4 In technology Dareen has designed three packages to hold a litre of juice.

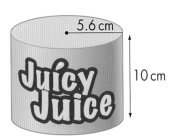

DESIGN 1

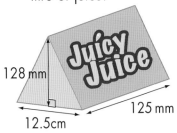

DESIGN 2

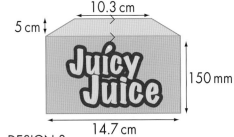

DESIGN 3

Consider each of the three designs and comment on the suitability of each.

5 An Olympic pool design is 25 metres wide and 50 metres long. The pool is 3 metres deep at the starting end of the pool and slopes up to 2 metres deep at the far end of the pool.

a What is the volume of the pool?

b Assuming the pool is full of water, how many litres of water will the pool contain?

Discussion 14.4

Have you ever been asked which is heavier – 1 kg of feathers or 1 kg of lead?

The answer is neither – they both have the same mass of 1 kg. Sometimes people are hard to convince. What they mean is that lead is **denser** than feathers. Can you explain what this means?

Density is a measure of the relationship between the mass of an object and the volume it occupies. Density refers to the mass per unit volume of a substance. It is calculated by using the formula

Density = Mass ÷ Volume.

$$D = \frac{M}{V}$$

The S.I. unit of density is the **kilogram per cubic metre (kg/m³)**.

For example, the density of air is 1.3 kg/m³. This means that 1 cubic metre of air has a mass of 1.3 kg.

For smaller volumes the unit of density is **grams per cubic centimetre (g/cm³)**.

Discussion 14.5

Describe how you could calculate your own density.

Why is it possible to float on top of the Dead Sea?

Example 14.3

A piece of copper has a volume of 8 cubic centimetres and a mass of 72 g. Find the density of copper.

Using the formula $\quad D = \frac{M}{V}$

$$D = 72\,g \div 8\,cm^3$$

$$D = 9\,g/cm^3$$

This means that a piece of copper of 1 cm³ has a mass of 9 g.

The density formula can be rearranged to find the mass of an object or its volume.

$$D = \frac{M}{V} \qquad \text{so } M = D \times V \quad \text{and} \quad V = \frac{M}{D}$$

Example 14.4

A piece of copper has a density of $9\,\text{g/cm}^3$ and a volume of $10\,\text{cm}^3$. Find its mass.

Using $\quad M = D \times V$

$\qquad\qquad M = 9\,\text{g/cm}^3 \times 10\,\text{cm}^3$

$\qquad\qquad M = 90\,\text{g}$

Example 14.5

A piece of copper has a mass of $45\,\text{g}$ and a density of $9\,\text{g/cm}^3$. What is its volume?

Using $\quad V = \frac{M}{D}$

$\qquad\qquad V = 45\,\text{g} \div 9\,\text{g/cm}^3$

$\qquad\qquad V = 5\,\text{cm}^3$

Exercise 14e

1 Use the formula to complete the table of densities of common substances.

Substance	Mass (g)	Volume (cm³)	Density (g/cm³)
Silver	21	2	
Steel	27.3	3.5	
Lead	678	60	
Blood	1600	1000	
Tin	1825	250	
Sugar	1000	625	
Oak	1400	2000	
Balsa Wood	36	300	
Pure water	267	267	

2 A glass window has a mass of 5 kg and a volume of 2000 cubic centimetres. Find the density of glass in g/cm³.

3 The density of gold is 19 g/cm³. A gold coin has a mass of 76 g.

   a What is its volume?

   b Another gold coin has a volume of 6 cm³. How much heavier is it than the first coin?

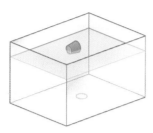

4 An object will only sink in a liquid of lower density than its own. Jill decides to carry out calculations to see if the following objects will sink or float in water. Carry out the calculations and help Jill decide. The density of water is 1.0 g/cm³.

   a Bottle having a mass of 354 g and a volume of 500 ml

   b A brick with a mass of 2268 g and a volume of 1230 cm³

   c A silver ring with a mass of 10.5 g and a volume of 1 cm³

   d A cork with a mass of 2 g and a volume of 4 cm³

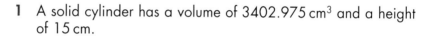

Consolidation Exercise

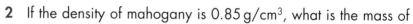

1 A solid cylinder has a volume of 3402.975 cm³ and a height of 15 cm.

   a Calculate the radius, r, of the circular end of the cylinder. Take π as 3.14.

   b Find the area of the circular base of the cylinder. Round the answer to three significant figures.

2 If the density of mahogany is 0.85 g/cm³, what is the mass of

   a 1 cm³   b 2 cm³   c 10 cm³ of mahogany?

3 What volume of wood is required to make this knife block?

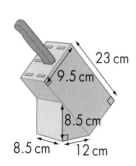

23 cm
9.5 cm
8.5 cm
8.5 cm   12 cm

4 The mass of air in a classroom measuring 10 m by 5 m by 2 m is 130 kg. What is the density of air in kg/m³?

5 A school eco-group has decided to recycle bean cans. The diameter of a can is 74 mm and the height is 10.7 cm.

   a Find the volume of a tin to the nearest cubic centimetre. Take π as 3.14.

   b The tin can be crushed to a volume of 240.72 cm³. Assuming the area of the base remains unchanged, find the height of the crushed tin to the nearest tenth of a centimetre.

Task 4: Planning applications

SUSTask 4

The local council has introduced a new building regulation which states that you will need planning permission to erect a structure or building of **more than 10 cubic metres** in your garden. This regulation applies to structures such as sheds, summer-houses, greenhouses, swimming pools and garden tunnels.

Part A

As part of the planning team, your role is to consider each of the applications on SUSTask4 and decide whether or not planning permission is necessary.

Application 1   **Child's playhouse**

Application 2   **Summer house**

Application 3   **Lean-to greenhouse**

Application 4   **Stand alone greenhouse**

Application 5   **Wooden shed**

Application 6   **Metal garden shed**

Application 7   **Grower system garden tunnel**

Application 8   **Red playhouse**

Application 9   **Kennel**

Application 10   **Swimming pool**

Part B

The regulation has been revised for garden sheds, summer houses and all other garden buildings. These are exempt from the regulation in Part A if the floor area of the building is **less than 15 m²**.

Will this amendment to the regulations affect any of the applications in Part A?

Percentages

In this chapter, I am learning to:

- express one number as a percentage of another
- calculate percentage increase and decrease
- carry out calculations for simple and compound interest.

Discussion 15.1

Ashlene wants to compare her last three exam results in maths. In Year 8 she scored $\frac{23}{40}$, in Year 9 $\frac{36}{60}$ and Year 10 $\frac{58}{95}$. What is the problem with these results when it comes to comparing them? What would it be sensible to do with her results? How can 23 be written as a percentage of 40? Use a calculator to find this result as a percentage, correct to the nearest whole number.

Similarly, convert Ashlene's other scores into percentages. What rule could be used to express any number, x as a percentage of another number, y? What is 200 m as a percentage of 1 km?

Is 36 as a percentage of 72 the same as 72 as a percentage of 36? Explain your answer.

Example 15.1

a Express 7 as a percentage of 35.

b Express 83 days as a percentage of 365 days correct to three significant figures.

a $\frac{7}{35} \times 100\% = \frac{1}{5} \times 100\% = 20\%$ (simplify the fraction first, where possible)

b

$$\boxed{8}\,\boxed{3}\,\boxed{\div}\,\boxed{3}\,\boxed{6}\,\boxed{5}\,\boxed{=}\,\boxed{\times}\,\boxed{1}\,\boxed{0}\,\boxed{0}\,\boxed{=}$$

22.73972603… = 22.7% (3 s.f.)

83 days = 22.7% of 365 days (3 s.f.)

Exercise 15a

1 Express the first number as a percentage of the second.

   a 30, 120   **b** 108, 144   **c** 63, 180   **d** 32, 400

   e 12, 30   **f** 17, 10

2 a What is 28 as a percentage of 40?

   b Give 0.8 as a percentage of 3.2.

3 a Write £9 as a percentage of £12.

   b Write 20 kg as a percentage of 200 kg.

   c Write 7 mm as a percentage of 20 mm.

4 Mrs Green spends £15 in the supermarket. If she spends £6 on vegetables, what percentage of her spending is on vegetables?

5 Express these as percentages.

   a £3 of £20   b 54 cm of 60 cm   c 880 kg of 1 tonne

   d 75p of £3   e 5 mm of 4 cm   f 84 cm of 2 m

   g 550 g of 2.5 kg   h 850 m of 5 km

Exercise 15b

1 Calculate, giving your answer correct to two decimal places where appropriate

   a 12 as a percentage of 27   b 55 as a percentage of 60

   c 1.2 as a percentage of 5.

2 Express these marks as percentages accurate to three significant figures.

   a 59 out of 70   b 23 out of 30   c 98 out of 160

   d 11 out of 24

3 Express these values as percentages accurate to two decimal places where appropriate.

   a 2.5 litres of 3 litres   b 8.5 hours of a day

   c 5 months of a year   d 83 minutes of $1\frac{1}{2}$ hours

4 Stirling brought his car to a mechanic to prepare it for its MOT. His bill came to £178.95. If the parts totalled £86.15 what is this as a percentage of the total? Give your answer to the nearest whole number percentage.

5 A football club increased its stadium capacity from 9950 to 14 775. What is the new capacity expressed as a percentage of the old capacity? Give your answer to two significant figures.

Total Weight: 400g
Meat content: 170g

Total Weight: 180g
Meat content: 75g

6 Which meat pie has the higher percentage content of meat?

7 The average monthly rainfall in Belfast, recorded over a number of years, is shown in the table.

Month	Dec	Jan	Feb	Mar	Apr	May	Jun	Jul	Aug	Sep	Oct	Nov
Rainfall (mm)	90	80	52	50	48	52	68	94	77	80	83	72
Season		Winter			Spring			Summer			Autumn	

a Express each month's rainfall as a percentage of the total annual rainfall.

b Express each season's rainfall as a percentage of the total annual rainfall. Comment on your findings.

8 In a sale a games console was reduced from £120 to £102. What is this reduction as a percentage of the original price?

Activity 15.1

Activity Sheet 15.1

Activity 15.2

Activity Sheet 15.2

Discussion 15.2

Nathan earns £510 per week. He is offered a pay rise of 4%. What non-calculator method could you use to find his weekly pay increase? Discuss your ideas with a partner. What is Nathan's increased weekly pay? What percentage of his original pay is this increased amount? What would be the most efficient way to use your calculator to find Nathan's new weekly pay?

Jean is confused. A shop advertises an MP3 player. Jean thinks the price is reduced to £80 and to check her answer she adds 20% back on as follows. 10% of £80 is £8, so 20% of £80 is £16.

£80 + £16 = £96. This is not the answer Jean expected. Can you explain her mistake?

What does **appreciate** mean in terms of value? Give an example of something whose value appreciates.

What does **depreciate** mean in terms of value? Give an example of something whose value depreciates year on year.

Example 15.2

A PC game costs £39.99. In a sale it has 35% off.
What is its reduced price?

As the game has been reduced by 35% the price paid is 65% of £39.99.

£39.99 × 0.65 = £25.99 to the nearest penny

Exercise 15c

1 Work out the following percentage increases and decreases **without using a calculator**.

a increase £340 by 3%   b decrease £15 000 by 15%

c increase 63 000 spectators by 8%

d reduce 26 cm by 30%   e increase 28.4 kg by 7%

f reduce 1.1 by 12%

2 A house was sold in 2005 for £154 000.

a The estate agent charged a 0.75% fee. What was the estate agent's fee?

The house's value appreciated 23% over the next two years.

b What was its value in 2007?

c It then lost 18.5% of its 2007 value over the next year. What was its value in 2008?

3 Jim bought a classic car for £7750. It appreciated in value by 11% over the course of the next year. What was its new value?

4 Ivan's shares depreciated in value by 43% during 2008. If his shares were valued at £17 403 at the end of 2007, what were they worth one year later?

5 Priscilla earns £32 000 a year. Deductions amount to 23.6% of her salary. What is her pay after deductions?

6 Hector's house contents are valued at £37 750. His insurance company charges a premium of 0.8% of the value insured. How much insurance does he pay?

7 Last year Alex's season ticket for his local football club cost £399. This year the price has risen by 4.6%. What is the increased price?

8 Mildred's car insurance premium rose from £422.65 a year by 127% after a series of accidents. What was her increased insurance premium?

9 One hundred years ago the population of Belfast was 405 000. Today it has declined by 15.5%. What is its population today?

10 VAT is charged on most goods and services. Find the VAT inclusive prices for each of the items below if VAT is **a** 17.5%, **b** 15%.

The prices which follow are exclusive of VAT.

i a clock costing £29

ii a holiday costing £1795

iii a computer costing £475

iv a drum kit costing £779.99

v a gold chain costing £54.75

vi a digital camera costing £37.89

vii a widescreen plasma TV costing £1149

viii a new car costing £23 790

ix a pencil costing 27p

x an eraser costing 7p

Discussion 15.3

Last year Sinead's youth club had 50 members. This year it has 58 members. How many extra members have joined? What is this increase as a percentage of the original 50 members? This is the percentage increase in membership.

Jenny is trying to find the percentage reduction in a sale where a blouse is reduced from £40 to £30. She isn't sure whether the answer is

$\frac{10}{40} \times 100\% = 25\%$ or $\frac{10}{30} \times 100\% = 33\frac{1}{3}\%$. What do you think?

Describe a rule to help you calculate percentage change. What is the percentage appreciation of an antique vase purchased for £70 and sold at auction for £84?

$$\text{Percentage change} = \frac{\text{difference}}{\text{original}} \times \mathbf{100\%}$$

Note: the difference is always a positive amount and is the difference between the original and the new value.

Example 15.3

A coat originally costing £105 is for sale at £80. What is the percentage reduction in price?

The original value is £105. The new value is £80. So the percentage change is

$\frac{105 - 80}{105} \times 100\% = 23.8\%$ to one decimal place.

Exercise 15d

1   What is the percentage depreciation of a new car costing £12 000 which loses £2400 of its value in its first six months?

2   What is the percentage appreciation of a stamp bought for £32 and sold for £49?

3   What is the percentage profit on a kitchen costing a manufacturer £3500 to produce which is then sold for £5275?

4   What is the percentage loss on a bicycle bought for £299 and later sold for £212?

5   **a** What is the percentage change on each of these amounts? State whether the change is a profit or loss.

	Original value	New value
i	£40	£48
ii	£6.77	£6
iii	23p	24p
iv	£178000	£202 500
v	£165.95	£120
vi	£47.60	£35
vii	£35	£47.60

   b Look at your answers to **vi** and **vii**. Is this what you expect? Explain why the percentage changes should be different.

6   By switching electrical items off rather than leaving them on standby the Power family's quarterly electricity bill fell from £106.53 to £92.71. What is their percentage saving?

7   **a** Max spent 52 minutes travelling to work in the morning and 47 minutes travelling home in the evening. As a percentage how much shorter was his return journey?

   b Wilma spent 1 hour and 15 minutes travelling to work in the morning and 1 hour 35 minutes travelling home in the evening. As a percentage how much longer was her return journey?

8   Safeco, a supermarket, produces its own bread for 47p a loaf. During a marketing campaign it sells its bread for 32p a loaf as a loss leader.

   a Why would the supermarket sell its bread at a loss?

   b What is its percentage loss on each loaf sold?

9   Jim buys a painting at a car boot sale for £13 and later sells it to an art collector for £340. What is his percentage profit?

10 Jules estimated 28 × 51 as 30 × 50 = 1500. The exact answer is 1428. What was Jules' percentage error (based on the exact answer)?

Activity
Sheet 15.3

Activity 15.3

Activity 15.4

Activity
Sheet 15.4

Discussion 15.4

Tony borrows £120 from his uncle Paulie and pays him back at £10 each month for a year. How much does he repay? Silvio borrows £1000 from his bank and pays back £90 each month for a year. How much does he repay? The bank has charged Silvio interest on the loan. Why does it do this? What is the rate of interest charged by the bank on Silvio's loan?

Banks and building societies loan money to companies and private individuals. There is an element of risk involved to the bank or building society. What risks can you think of?

Apart from personal loans to pay for new cars, holidays and decorating homes, many people also have a mortgage. What is a mortgage used to pay for?

Would you expect the interest rate banks charge for loans to be the same as the rate of interest they pay to savers?

Carmela has a savings account with her bank. Her savings earn 2% interest per annum. How much would her £5000 savings earn in a year? How much interest would be earned in three years if the interest rate remains at 2%?

This method of calculating interest is known as **simple interest**. Simple interest is always calculated on the initial investment (**principal amount**). In Carmela's case she has a total of £5100 after one year. In her second year of saving she still earns interest at a rate of 2% on her principal amount of £5000, not on her accumulated savings of £5100. So after two years Carmela will have £5200 in her account and £5300 after three years.

Example 15.4

Mr Barclay invests £3700 into a savings plan which pays 3.5% simple interest per annum. How much is his investment worth after **a** one year **b** three years?

a Find 3.5% of £3700

Calculator method 1: 0.035 × £3700 = £129.50;
£3700 + £129.50 = £3829.50

Calculator method 2: 1.035 × £3700 = £3829.50

b The amount of interest earned in year 1 is also earned in years 2 and 3.

£129.50 × 3 = £388.50; after 3 years the value of Mr Barclay's investment is £3700 + £388.50 = £4088.50

Exercise 15e

1 Find the simple interest accrued (earned) for the given principal amounts invested as follows:

	Principal amount	Time	Interest rate (per annum)
a	£250	1 year	4%
b	£1075	2 years	5.5%
c	£6600	3 years	7%
d	£95	4 years	4.75%
e	£3750	5 years	6.89%

2 Mr Paribas keeps £720 for three years in an account earning 6% simple interest per annum. What is the value of his savings at the end of the three-year period?

3 Miss Westminster invested £2000 in a savings account for one year. At the end of the year her savings had grown to £2150. What rate of simple interest did she earn?

4 Abbey invested £500 in a savings account for three years. At the end of three years her investment was worth £680. What rate of simple interest did she earn per annum?

5 How long does it take for a sum of £300 to earn £72 simple interest at 6% per annum?

Activity Sheet 15.5

Activity 15.5

Discussion 15.5

What is a debit card? What is a credit card?

Credit card companies insist on minimum monthly repayments based on a percentage of the amount outstanding. For example, a company may state in its terms and conditions that minimum monthly repayments are made of 5% of the amount outstanding or £5, whichever is greater. Priscilla's credit card bill is £540. What is 5% of her outstanding amount? What is the minimum amount Priscilla must repay? Prudence receives a £37 credit card bill. What is her minimum repayment?

Exercise 15f

1. Sally receives her credit card bill. Her outstanding balance is £102.45. What is her minimum repayment if she must pay either 2.95% of her bill or £3 whichever is larger?

2. Lawrence owes £903.59 on his credit card. What is his minimum repayment if he must pay either 5.15% or £20, whichever is the greater?

3. Andrew buys a second-hand car on credit. He pays a deposit of £500 and 36 monthly repayments of £125.

   a. What is the total amount paid for the car?

   b. If the car had a cash price of £4250, how much interest was paid?

   c. Express the interest paid as a percentage of the cash price.

4. Neil buys a new flat for £205 000. He pays a £25 000 deposit and takes out a mortgage for the remainder of the price. His mortgage is taken out over 25 years and his monthly repayments are £1270.

   a. What is the the total cost of the flat?

   b. What is the amount of interest paid?

   c. Express the interest paid as a percentage of the amount borrowed.

5. Sean owes £2000 on his credit card. The bank adds interest at a rate of 3% each month. Sean repays £250 each month.

   a. Copy and complete this table.

Month	Interest charged (3%)	Amount owed	Amount repaid	Amount owed
1	3% of £2000 = £60	£2060	£250	£2060 – £250 = £1810
2	3% of £1810 =			
3				

   b. How much does Sean repay in three months?

   c. How much has Sean's debt decreased by in three months?

6. Bill purchased a new computer costing £825 on credit terms. He signs a credit agreement where he will make 24 payments of £39.95 a month by direct debit.

   a. What is the total price Bill pays for the computer?

   b. How much interest is he charged?

   c. Express the interest charged as a percentage of the cost price.

Discussion 15.6

Simple interest is a type of interest which isn't used very often these days. **Compound interest** is used by banks, building societies and shops. If £1000 is invested for two years at 10% simple interest the interest earned is £100 each year. After one year the investment is worth £1100 and the total value of the investment after two years is £1200.

If the same amount is invested for two years at 10% compound interest, the interest added each year does not remain at £100. After one year the investment is still worth £1100, but in the second year the interest earned is 10% of £1100, which is £110. What is the total value of the investment after two years? Explain the difference between simple and compound interest.

Jean invests £2000 at 10% compound interest for a period of three years. What is her investment worth after one year? What is it worth after two years? What is it worth after three years? How much more money is earned over the three years by applying compound rather than simple interest to the principal amount?

Example 15.5

Find the interest earned on an investment of £1500 for three years at 5% compound interest.

Interest earned in first year: 5% of £1500 = £75

Value of investment after one year = £1500 + £75 = £1575

Interest earned in second year: 5% of £1575 = £78.75

Value of investment after two years = £1575 + £78.75 = £1653.75

Interest earned in third year: 5% of £1653.75 = £82.69 (to the nearest penny)

Value of investment after three years = £1653.75 + £82.69 = £1736.44

Total interest earned = £1736.44 – £1500 = £236.44

Exercise 15g

1 The following principal amounts are invested at the given rates of compound interest. Find the final value of the investments at the end of the time period given.

	Principal amount	Time	Interest rate (per annum)
a	£200	2 years	4%
b	£1075	2 years	7%
c	£6000	3 years	9%
d	£105	3 years	4.75%
e	£13500	3 years	5.89%

2 What is the total interest paid on savings of £560 invested for two years at 6% compound interest?

3 What is the total interest paid on savings of £3300 invested for three years at 4% compound interest?

4 What is the total interest paid on savings of £15 000 invested for three years at 5.5% compound interest?

5 Julie borrows £3000 over three years at 10% compound interest per annum.

 a How much does she repay in total?

 b What is the total interest paid?

 c Express the interest as a percentage of the amount borrowed.

 d Julie pays her loan back in equal monthly instalments. How much does she repay each month to the nearest penny?

6 £445 is invested for two years at 3.75% compound interest. How much interest is earned?

7 Cathy borrows £700 which she agrees to repay over two years at 7.49% compound interest. What is the total cost of her loan?

8 Percy wants to invest £4400 for two years.

 a Find the interest he would receive if he invested the money at 6% simple interest.

 b Find the interest he would receive if he invested the money at 5% compound interest.

 c Which investment is better and by how much?

9 Which is the more profitable way to invest £20 000 for 3 years: 8.75% simple interest or 8.25% compound interest per annum?

10 Find the difference between simple and compound interest on an investment of £365 for three years at 5.05% per annum.

Activity 15.6

Activity
Sheet 15.6

Activity 15.7

Activity
Sheet 15.7

Consolidation Exercise

1 Express these marks as percentages.

   a 28 out of 40   b 27 out of 60   c 98 out of 140

   d 13 out of 20   e 23 out of 25   f 175 out of 250

2 Sophie borrows £7000 over 60 months. Her repayments are £160 per month.

   a What is the total cost of Sophie's loan?

   b How much interest is she charged?

   c Express the interest charged as a percentage of the amount borrowed.

3 Jamie entered a javelin competition. His first throw was 46 m. His second throw was 3% further and his final throw 5% further still.

   a How far was Jamie's second throw?

   b How far was his final throw?

   c Jamie's personal best javelin throw is 51 m. What is his final throw as a percentage of his personal best?

4 Jim owes £86.59 to his credit card company. What is his minimum repayment if he must pay either 4.75% of the outstanding balance or £5, whichever is the greater?

5 What is 115% of £12?

6 A new computer is advertised at £499 + VAT or £579 including VAT. Which is the better deal if **a** VAT is 17.5%, **b** VAT is 15%?

7 Morgan and Stanley open building society accounts. The building society offers these savings rates.

Amount	Interest rate per annum
Up to £1000	3.5%
£1001–£5000	4.5%
Over £5000	5.5%

Morgan invests £950 and Stanley £4400 over three years.

a How much simple interest will they each earn?

b How much extra would be earned if they invested their combined total of £5350 into a single account?

8 What is the final value of a £370 investment at 5.19% compound interest over a period of three years?

9 Which of the options below provides the better investment opportunity and by how much?

Option 1: Invest £500 at 9.99% compound interest for three years.

Option 2: Invest £500 at 10.65% simple interest for three years.

Task 5: Computer calculations

Part A

Sid buys a new computer. He was careful to specify the individual components that he wanted and a breakdown of the cost of his new PC cost is given.

Component	Price
Processor: Intel Core 2 Quad-Core Q8200	£143.62
Operating system: Windows Vista Home Premium	£86.62
Monitor: 19" Widescreen TFT	£93.14
Memory: 2048MB 800MHz Dual Channel DDR2 SDRAM	£29.77
Hard drive: 320GB (7200rpm) SATA Hard Drive	£35.56
Graphics card: 256MB ATI Radeon HD 3450	£25.20
Optical drives: DVD+/–RW Drive	£15.28
Keyboard/Mouse: Wireless	£55.80
Speakers: 5.1 Digital speakers	£34.49
Cabling, case, fan, labour	£79.52

Write the price of each component as a percentage of the total cost. Comment on your findings.

Part B

You have £730 to buy a new PC. Some conditions, however, have been imposed as follows:

- no more than 30% of the total price may be spent on the processor
- at least 7% of the total price must be spent on memory
- no more than 25% of the total price must be spent on the monitor
- at least 15% of the total price must be spent on the graphics card
- cabling, case, fan and labour cost £79.52.

Use the website www.scan.co.uk to choose your components. Copy and complete the table.

Component	Model	Price	Percentage of overall cost
Processor			
Operating system			
Monitor			
Memory			
Hard drive			
Graphics card			
Optical drive			
Keyboard/Mouse			
Speakers			
Cabling, case, fan, labour		£79.52	

Give reasons for your choices.

16 Probability

In this chapter, I am learning to:

- express the probability of an event happening as a percentage, fraction or decimal
- show the outcomes of two events using lists, two-way tables and tree diagrams
- understand and calculate relative frequency
- compare the outcomes of experimental and theoretical probability and understand that different outcomes may occur in experimental probability.

$$\text{probability of an outcome} = \frac{\text{number of ways the outcome can happen}}{\text{total number of possible outcomes}}$$

Example 16.1

Calculate the probability of obtaining a head when tossing a fair coin.

The probability of tossing a head on a coin $P(H) = \frac{1}{2}$ because there are two possible outcomes but only one way of obtaining a head.

$$\text{probability of a head} = \frac{\text{number of heads}}{\text{total number of possible outcomes}}$$

Exercise 16a

Give your answers in this exercise as fractions in their simplest form.

1 In a class of 31 pupils, six have blonde hair, 12 brown hair, two ginger hair, seven black hair and four have dyed hair. One of the pupils is chosen at random.

What is the probability of the pupil having

a brown hair   b dyed hair   c blonde or ginger hair?

2 Miss Jones asks a pupil in her class to be the form monitor. There are 18 girls in the class and 13 boys. She chooses a pupil at random.

a What is the probability that she will choose a girl from the class?

b What is the probability that she will choose a boy from the class?

c What is the probability that Miss Jones will choose a boy or girl from the class?

3 John pulls a sock out of his drawer which contains three red socks, five black socks and two white socks. If the sock is selected at random, find the probability that the sock is
a black b white c red.

d Show that the probability of picking a sock from the drawer is equal to 1.

4 A letter is chosen at random from the word PROBABILITY. What is the probability of choosing

a the letter T

b a vowel

c a consonant

d the letter I

e the letter E?

5 A bag of fruit sweets contains six strawberry, three lemon, five lime and seven raspberry.

a A sweet is chosen at random and the probability of choosing this flavour is $\frac{1}{3}$. What flavour is it?

b Joe says that the probability of choosing a strawberry sweet at random is $\frac{1}{7}$. Is he correct? Give a reason to support your answer.

Discussion 16.1

The weather forecaster says that the probability of rain today is going to be 75%. Jane cannot decide whether to take her umbrella or not. What would you advise?

What is the probability that it will not rain?

12pm Tuesday

The probability of snow in January is $\frac{1}{3}$

This can be written as **P(snow) = $\frac{1}{3}$**.

P(event happening) + P(event not happening) = 1

Since probabilities for an event always add up to 1, then

P(no snow) = 1 − $\frac{1}{3}$ = $\frac{2}{3}$

Exercise 16b

1 The probability that Rachel will get up early is 0.4. What is the probability that she will not get up early?

2 The probability of Jan winning a race on sports day is 43%. What is the probability she will not win this race?

3 The probability that there will be no pupils absent from school on Monday is 0.67. What is the probability that there will be at least one pupil absent on Monday?

4 The probability of throwing a six on a biased die is 0.25. What is the probability that the number on the die will not be six?

5 Scott places 15 pieces of paper, numbered from 1 to 15, in a hat. He chooses a number at random from the hat.

   a What is the probability of choosing an even number?

   b What is the probability of choosing an odd number?

   c What is P(prime number)?

   d What is P(number which is not prime)?

6 A bag contains red, blue and green beads. A bead is picked from the bag at random. If P(red) = $\frac{13}{20}$ and P(blue) = $\frac{3}{20}$, what is:

   a P(green)   b P(not red)

   c P(yellow)   d P(not blue)?

7 The school bus can arrive early, on time or late.

   The probability that the school bus arrives on time is 0.34.

   The probability that the school bus is late is 0.23.

   a What is the probability that the school bus will be early?

   b What is the probability that the bus will not be late?

   c What is the probability that the bus will not arrive on time?

Discussion 16.2

Gavin and his friend are trying to work out how many different outcomes are possible when two dice are thrown together. Gavin says there are 21 ways while his friend argues that the answer is 36. Can you work out how both boys arrived at their answers? Who do you think is correct?

Finding all the possible outcomes can be difficult when dealing with more than one event, for example, tossing two dice, so it is important to have a systematic approach.

When more than one event takes place, there are different ways of recording all the possible outcomes. The outcomes may be written as a **list** or as **a space diagram.**

Writing the outcomes as a list we have

1, 1	1, 2	1, 3	1, 4	1, 5	1, 6
2, 1	2, 2	2, 3	2, 4	2, 5	2, 6
3, 1	3, 2	3, 3	3, 4	3, 5	3, 6
4, 1	4, 2	4, 3	4, 4	4, 5	4, 6
5, 1	5, 2	5, 3	5, 4	5, 5	5, 6
6, 1	6, 2	6, 3	6, 4	6, 5	6, 6

A space diagram can also be referred to as **a two–way table.** The outcomes of the two events are represented as rows and columns.

		Second die					
		1	**2**	**3**	**4**	**5**	**6**
	1	1, 1	1, 2	1, 3	1, 4	**1, 5**	1, 6
	2	2, 1	2, 2	2, 3	**2, 4**	2, 5	2, 6
First	**3**	3, 1	3, 2	**3, 3**	3, 4	3, 5	3, 6
die	**4**	4, 1	**4, 2**	4, 3	4, 4	4, 5	4, 6
	5	**5, 1**	5, 2	5, 3	5, 4	5, 5	5, 6
	6	6, 1	6, 2	6, 3	6, 4	6, 5	6, 6

When two dice are tossed there are a total of **36** possible outcomes.

The probability of obtaining a total score of 6 on the two dice is $\frac{5}{36}$ as there are **five** different ways to obtain a total of six.

These have been highlighted in the space diagram.

Exercise 16c

	Coin 1	
Coin 2	H	T
H		
T		

1 Draw a space diagram to show all the possible outcomes when two coins are tossed.

   a How many possible outcomes are there?

   b What is P(both coins show heads)?

   c What is P(no coins show heads)?

   d Which outcome occurs most often?

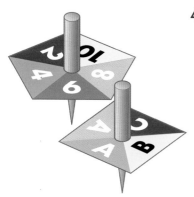

Second die

+	1	2	3	4	5	6
1	2	3	4	5	6	7
2						
3						
4						
5						
6						

First die

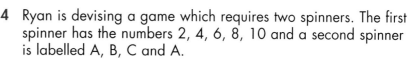

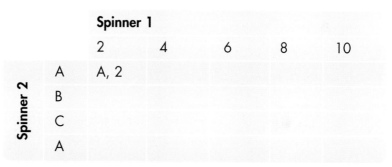

2 a Draw a space diagram to show the total score obtained when two dice are thrown at the same time and the scores added together. The first row of the table has been completed for you.

Use the completed space diagram to find

b P(total score of 12)   **c** P(1)   **d** P(6)

e P(obtaining a number which is a multiple of 4)

f P(obtaining a number which is divisible by 6)

3 On a school menu there are four main courses and four desserts.

List all the different possible combinations I can choose for main course and dessert.

MENU
Main Course
Pizza
Burger
Baked potato
Curry

Dessert
Yoghurt
Custard
Apple tart
Sponge

4 Ryan is devising a game which requires two spinners. The first spinner has the numbers 2, 4, 6, 8, 10 and a second spinner is labelled A, B, C and A.

Ryan wishes to find all the possible outcomes which are possible when both spinners are spun once.

a Copy and complete the space diagram to show all the possible outcomes.

		Spinner 1				
		2	4	6	8	10
Spinner 2	A	A, 2				
	B					
	C					
	A					

b What is the probability of an outcome which does not contain the letter A?

c Ryan decides that an outcome of B,10 is needed to start the game. What is the probability of obtaining this outcome?

d Laura tells Ryan that the game would begin much quicker if he chose the letter A with any number. Is she correct? Give a reason to support your answer.

5 Two fair spinners are used in a game. The green spinner is marked with the numbers 1, 2, 3 and 4 and the blue spinner is numbered 1, 2 and 3. The two spinners are spun at the same time and the two scores are multiplied.

a Draw a two–way table to show all the possible multiplied scores.

b Calculate the probability of :

i obtaining an odd number

ii obtaining a multiple of 3

iii obtaining a multiple of 4

c To start the game Team A has to score a multiple of 4. In order for Team B to start they need a score which is a multiple of 6. Is this fair?

Activity Sheet 16.1

Activity 16.1

Another method used to show all the possible outcomes from an experiment is to draw a **tree diagram**. Each **branch** in the tree diagram represents a possible outcome.

This tree diagram shows all the outcomes when a coin is tossed twice.

FIRST TOSS	SECOND TOSS	OUTCOMES
$\frac{1}{2}$ H	$\frac{1}{2}$ H	HH
	$\frac{1}{2}$ T	HT
$\frac{1}{2}$ T	$\frac{1}{2}$ H	TH
	$\frac{1}{2}$ T	TT

From the tree diagram, it is easy to see that there are four possible outcomes: HH, HT, TH and TT. The probability of obtaining two tails = $\frac{1}{4}$.

Discussion 16.3

Look at the tree diagram on the previous page.

Consider the branches highlighted in red showing the outcomes from the first toss of the coin. What is the sum of the probabilities shown on the branches?

Consider the branches highlighted in green. What is the sum of the probabilities shown on the branches? Does this work for the orange branches?

Two events are called **independent** if the probability of the first event happening does not affect the probability of the second event. For example, when a coin is tossed twice and a head obtained on the first toss, the probability of obtaining a head on the second toss is not affected.

Exercise 16d

1 The probability of having to stop at a set of traffic lights is 0.75.

   a What is the probability of not having to stop at a set of traffic lights?

   b There are two independent sets of traffic lights on a stretch of road. Draw a tree diagram to show whether you need to stop at both sets of traffic lights.

2 A fair die is rolled twice in a game. A prize is won each time an odd number is obtained.

   a What is the probability of rolling the die and winning a prize on the first roll of the die? Give the answer in its simplest form.

   b What is the probability of rolling the die a second time and winning a prize? Give the answer in its simplest form.

   c What is the probability of rolling the die and not winning a prize **i** on the first roll and **ii** on the second roll?

   d Copy and complete the tree diagram.

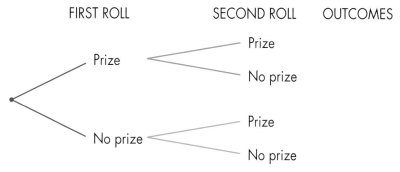

   e What is the probability of not winning a prize in the game after two rolls of the die?

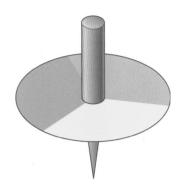

3 a Draw a tree diagram to represent a coin being tossed three times.

b Use the diagram to list all the possible outcomes.

c What is the probability of tossing three heads in a row?

4 A coin is tossed and at the same time this spinner is spun.

a Draw a tree diagram to show all the possible outcomes.

b What is the probability of tossing a tail and the spinner landing on yellow?

Discussion 16.4

Andy explains to his friend that the team can either win, lose or draw and since there are three possible outcomes, the P(win) = $\frac{1}{3}$. Is Andy correct?

Relative frequency of an outcome is not the probability that the event will happen but just an estimate of that probability from experimental data.

Relative frequency of an outcome can be calculated using the formula

relative frequency = $\dfrac{\text{number of times an event happens}}{\text{total number of outcomes}}$

When calculating relative frequency, a larger number of trials will obtain a more reliable result.

Exercise 16e

1 Look at each of the statements and decide if they are true or false. Explain your answer.

a The school canteen offers four flavours of drink – lemon, cola, raspberry and lime. The probability that Haley chooses lime is $\frac{1}{4}$.

b Graeme has a rubber, pen and pencil in his pocket. The probability of choosing the pen at random is $\frac{1}{3}$.

c Hailey's mum is having a baby. The probability of it being a boy is $\frac{1}{2}$.

d In a multi–pack of crisps there are three packets of bacon and three packets of salt and vinegar. Jill picks a bag at random. The probability of choosing bacon is $\frac{1}{2}$.

2 A bag contains a number of counters which are red, blue, green or yellow. When a counter is picked at random from the bag the probability of it being green is 0.15 and the probability of picking a blue counter is 0.35.

The probability of taking out a red counter is the same as the probability of taking out a yellow counter.

What is the probability of picking a red counter at random?

Marble colour	Frequency
Black	7
Green	4
Blue	3
Red	6

3 George has 20 marbles in a bag. His friend, Fred, randomly selects a marble from the bag and records the colour chosen. The marble is then replaced. Fred repeats this 20 times and the results are shown in the table.

a Fred tells George that there must be seven black marbles in the bag. Explain why Fred may be wrong.

b George says that he put a white marble into the bag. Fred says that it is impossible and George is telling a lie. Who would you agree with? Give a reason to support your answer.

c George tells Fred to repeat the experiment for another 20 trials. How may this affect the results in the table?

d Calculate the relative frequency of each marble colour as a decimal.

Character	Frequency
Bart Samson	46
Inspector Latchet	9
Scragy Dog	33
Bendy	12

4 Pete conducts a survey on favourite cartoon characters. The results are recorded in the table.

a How many people were surveyed?

b Calculate the relative frequency of each character as a fraction, decimal and percentage.

Activity Sheet 16.2

Activity 16.2

Relative frequency can be used to make estimates about a population.

Estimated size of a particular event (or outcome) = relative frequency × total population.

Example 16.2

A bag contains beads of different colours. 100 beads were drawn and 32 of them were green. The relative frequency of choosing a green bead is 0.32. If there are 150 beads in the bag, estimate the expected number of beads in the bag which are green.

The number of green beads can be estimated by multiplying the total population by the relative frequency.

Estimate of number of green beads = 0.32 × 150 = 48

It is estimated that there are 48 green beads in the bag.

Exercise 16f

1 A drawing pin can land 'tip up' or 'tip down'. When dropped 200 times it lands 'tip up' 68 times. Estimate the probability of the pin landing:

   a tip up   **b** tip down.

2 In a group of Year 10 pupils 56 pupils are right handed and 34 pupils are left handed. Estimate the probability of a pupil being chosen at random being:

   a left handed   **b** right handed.

Score	Frequency
1	27
2	36
3	39
4	24
5	3
6	21

3 A biased die is rolled 150 times and the results are recorded in a table.

   a Explain why the results indicate that the die is biased.

   b Calculate the relative frequency of obtaining each score on the die.

   c If the die is tossed 600 times, how many times would I expect to score a 5?

4 The relative frequency of rain in November was 0.8. Estimate the number of days it will rain next November.

5 A football team has won six, lost four and drawn in ten matches during the season. Estimate the probability that the team will win the next match that they play.

Activity 16.3

Activity Sheet 16.3

Consolidation Exercise

1 Sharon has a bag containing four toffees, three mints, five chocolates and four fruit sweets.

   She offers the bag to her friend Sue who picks a sweet at random.

   a What is the probability that Sue will choose a fruit sweet?

   b What is the probability that Sue will not pick a mint?

   c What is the probability that Sue will not pick a chocolate sweet?

   d Sue picks a toffee sweet and eats it. Sharon then picks a sweet at random. What is the probability that Sharon will pick a toffee?

2 In a basketball competition, the probability of the school team winning is 15%, and the probability of drawing is 39%.

   a What is the probability that the team will lose?

   b What is the probability that the match does not result in a draw?

3 In a particular school the probability of the next pupil to pass through the classroom door being a boy is 1. Can you suggest a reason for this?

4 Harry has one coin which he tosses three times. His results were H, T, H.

   a List all possible outcomes that could have occurred.

   b Calculate

      i   P(3H)   ii P(obtaining exactly 2H)

      iii P(no H)   iv P(2T, 1H)

5 Joe is playing a game with two identical coins which have STOP written on one side and GO written on the other side.

   a Draw a tree diagram to show all the possible outcomes when Joe tosses the first coin. Extend the tree diagram to show what happens when Joe tosses the second coin.

   b To start the game Joe needs to get GO written on both coins. What is the probability that Joe will obtain two GOs?

6 A computer firm makes computer disks. It tests a random sample from a large batch of disks and calculates that the probability of a disk being defective is 0.012.

   a What is the probability that a disk chosen at random is not defective?

   b A customer places an order for 5000 disks. Estimate the number of defective disks in this order.

7 In Northern Ireland the relative frequency of snow falling on the mountains in November is 0.15. Estimate the number of days in November that snow will fall on the mountains.

Task 6: Experimental probability

SUSTask 6

The aim of this task is to show that increasing trials brings experimental probability closer to theoretical probability.

Part A

In pairs roll and record dice outcomes for about five minutes. Use a table such as the one on SUSTask6 to record your results:

What is the relative frequency as a percentage for each outcome? Comment on your results. How could you improve them?

You may choose to display your results in an appropriate chart or diagram.

Part B

Collate class results and complete the second table on SUSTask6. What assumption must you make?

Comment on the cumulative results of the class.

Part C

Use the spreadsheet package to generate random numbers from 1 to 10 inclusive and check their 'randomness' by computing experimental probability and comparing against theoretical probability. Comment on what you notice.

Use a table like the third table on SUSTask6 for the instructions which follow.

Generate 100 random numbers and complete the first 3 columns.

Now generate a further 100 and complete the next columns.

Repeat this procedure, adding more columns to the spreadsheet as required, until you have results for 1000 trials.

Finally, increase your number of trials to at least 3000.

Comment on your findings and display your results using appropriate charts and diagrams.

Index